T0168064

Praise for *No City for Slow Men*

"Hong Kong lawyer and blogger Jason Y. Ng is back with a new book of insights after casting his perceptive gaze over the good, bad and ugly side of city life. He offers 36 nicely judged, pithy – often punchy – essays to 'inform and empower' readers. Ng's unpretentious writing reveals a frank, cut-to-the-chase view of life – plus, on occasion, a commendably sympathetic nature."

– Guy Haydon, *South China Morning Post*

"The most engrossing part of *No City for Slow Men* – and, indeed, Ng's writing in general – is his sincerity, laying bare the best and worst of Hong Kong society, as well as his own struggles and insecurities."

– Meredith McBride, *Time Out Hong Kong*

"*HKID* says it best: Hong Kong is stuck somewhere between the Chinese mainland and the rest of the world, and that causes a bit of an identity crisis. Another major theme is the contrast between the lives of expats and locals — with their gambling by way of cards instead of mahjong, the strange sport of rugby and lack of Cantonese fluency. The plight of the domestic worker is an especially important topic, written about with great heart."

– Ray Hecht, *Shenzhen Daily*

"At once critical and invitingly funny, Ng offers imaginative musings of the social and cultural problems facing Hong Kong while sharpening our senses about the city we inhabit."

– John Erni, professor, Department of Humanities and Creative Writing, Hong Kong Baptist University

"Ng's prose is marked by honesty, clarity and wit, and his book is full of insight and humor about a city and a people still coming to terms with who they are and who they want to be."

— Kent Ewing, *Asia Times*

"Jason strips Hong Kong naked so that we can see her beauty and her flaws. Caught in the right light, she is beautiful; in the wrong, ugly and past it. Her character is in turn charming and delightful, but also irrational and psychotic. *No City for Slow Men* is a great introduction to the now of Hong Kong, how it emerged, and its possible future."

— Lawrence Gray, chairman, the Hong Kong Writers' Circle

"Ng has done it again! His new book is as personal and insightful as the first. He writes that true love is about the little things, and that's how we feel about Hong Kong. For all its complexities and eccentricities, it is our home."

— Zeb Eckert, anchor, Bloomberg Television

"A masterful essayist and gifted wordsmith, Ng captures modern-day Hong Kong in this witty and authentic collection."

— Shonee Mirchandani, managing director, Bookazine

"What pulses through the chapters is Jason's love for Hong Kong and its people. An entertaining narrator, he gazes over the city with clarity, verve and wit, giving its natives and guests alike the same wondrous sense of discovery."

— Paul Tam, general manager, the Hong Kong International Literary Festival

"Ng writes with erudition and wit. His new book is a fine toothcomb running through our contemporary issues and obsessions, an essential read for Hong Kongers and all who are in love with our city!"
 — Douglas Young, artist, provocateur and founder of G.O.D.

"Ng's observations are compelling, entertaining and insightful. His essay 'Maid in Hong Kong' provides a much needed voice to the migrant worker community in Hong Kong."
 — Noel Servigon, Philippine Consul General to Hong Kong

"From petty annoyances to post-handover identity, Ng weaves the ultimate narrative through the unique nature of Hong Kong life. *No City for Slow Men* is a must-read for anyone who has ever set foot in the Fragrant Harbour."
 — Chris Thrall, author of *Eating Smoke*

Praise for *HONG KONG State of Mind*

"Honest, insightful and immensely entertaining."
 — Joseph Chow, editor-in-chief, *Elle (HK)*

"Refreshingly frank and wry observations on Hong Kong life."
 — Matthew Harrison, author of *Jessica's Choice*

"A thoughtful guy not shy about exposing what happens between his ears, Ng is a man of principle and daring."
 — *Cairns Media Magazine*

By the same author

❧ **Books** ☙

HONG KONG State of Mind:
37 Views of a City that Doesn't Blink

Umbrellas in Bloom:
Hong Kong's occupy movement uncovered

As We See It:
Hong Kong Stories
(contributor)

Queen of Statue Square:
New Short Fiction from Hong Kong
(contributor)

Hong Kong Future Perfect:
One City, Twenty Visions of What is to Come
(contributor)

❧ **Blogs/Columns** ☙

As I See It
www.asiseeithk.com

The Real Deal
www.realdealhk.com

South China Morning Post
www.scmp.com/author/jason-y-ng-1

Hong Kong Free Press
www.hongkongfp.com/author/jasonyng

No City for Slow Men

Hong Kong's Quirks and Quandaries Laid Bare

Jason Y. Ng

BLACKSMITH BOOKS

No City for Slow Men
ISBN 978-988-16138-7-5

The author would like to thank Lee Po Ng for the 44 magnificent illustrations featured in this volume; Jack Chang for appearing on the cover; Mark Herz, Louise Aitken and Pete Spurrier for their editorial support; the Foreign Correspondents' Club and Pacific Coffee where most of this volume was written; and last but not least, his readers and blog followers whose staunch support has made it all possible.

Illustrations by Lee Po Ng • Maps by Kelvin Ng
Cover design by Ada Ng • Cover photography by Jason Y. Ng

Published by Blacksmith Books
Unit 26, 19/F, Block B, Wah Lok Industrial Centre,
37-41 Shan Mei St, Fo Tan, Hong Kong
Tel: (+852) 2877 7899 • *www.blacksmithbooks.com*

For my parents,

whose pride is my sole motivation

That is no country for old men. The young
        In one another's arms, birds in the trees
Those dying generations – at their song
        The salmon-falls, the mackerel-crowded seas
Fish, flesh, or fowl, commend all summer long
        Whatever is begotten, born, and dies
Caught in that sensual music all neglect
        Monuments of unageing intellect

                     – William Butler Yeats
                     Sailing to Byzantium

What is a city, but the people
True the people are the city.

                     – William Shakespeare
                     Coriolanus III

Sometimes life is kind and sweet
        Sometimes life is fraught with fears
Under the Lion Rock we meet
        And hope for more laughs than tears

                     – James Wong
                     Under the Lion Rock

Contents

Part 3 – Our Identity

Introduction

Writing a book is like having a baby. It is exhilarating and emotional. It is also laborious and mentally trying. The author must slug through the manuscript line by line, page after page. The process has to be repeated many times over until it finally comes out of the womb of the press. Once published, the labor of love takes on a life on its own. It will grow, stumble and then pick itself up. But a parent's love is unconditional – whatever the reception, the author will always be the book's biggest fan.

Continuing with that metaphor, writing a second book is akin to getting pregnant again. The perils facing the second child are well known: the novelty of parenthood is gone, comparison with the first born is inevitable. Though many second-time parents discover just the opposite. They discover that, as the family grows, their love multiplies rather than divides. It is one of those human experiences that defies logic and explanation. As I am putting the finishing touches on my second volume here at my favorite café overlooking Hollywood Road, that about sums up how I feel.

No City for Slow Men is a follow-up to *HONG KONG State of Mind*, released in December 2010 to warm reviews. A lot has happened in Hong Kong in the three years since then. The city has a new chief executive, the Apple Store opened three locations, property prices almost doubled. The overhang of a global financial crisis has dissipated, only to give way to deeper systemic issues. Poverty, a housing shortage and racial disharmony have polarized and paralyzed our society. Distrust of government and big business has surged to new highs. Tensions between Hong Kong and mainland China are boiling over. So what are we to do?

The first step in tackling any problem is admitting there is one. The second step is paying attention. In *The Art of War*, General Sun Tze teaches us to know our enemies and know ourselves. This book is intended to do just that. It brings into sharp focus a range of social, cultural and existential quandaries facing our society. It is a collection of opinions that cut through the obfuscation and get straight to the point. It aims to inform and empower.

It also aims to entertain. Hong Kong may be short on land and patience, but there is no scarcity of oddities that tickle us pink. Two books in and I have barely scratched the surface. Our quirks are in such abundance that I could easily write another two dozen volumes. Short of treading into Octomom territory, that is perhaps where the metaphor of child birth will end.

Throughout our history, we have been told time and again that we are a city in decline. Skeptics have long prophesized the end of Hong Kong. Plight after predicament, we have proven them wrong. Our optimism, resilience and that copyrightable brand of Lion Rock Spirit have always pulled us out of the rut. It is ever thus.

Jason Y. Ng
Hong Kong, 2014

About the Illustrator

Born in the town of Toishan, Guangdong, Lee Po Ng followed his mother to Hong Kong during the Chinese Civil War. Ng quit school at the age of 15 to become an apprentice to a local painter and spent the next four decades working as a freelance cartoonist and illustrator under the aliases Szema Yu (司馬瑜) and Yut Dor (一多).

In the 1960s, Lee Po Ng tried his hand at editing and went on to launch a daily newspaper with a group of like-minded friends. Refusing to trade his paintbrushes for a pen, Ng continued to tread the unbeaten path of a newspaper illustrator. His artistic career peaked in the 1980s during the hey day of the print media, contributing to as many as 15 newspapers, among which *Ming Pao* and the *Sing Tao Daily* are still in circulation today.

Ng now resides in Toronto, Canada with his family. He splits his time between teaching art and practicing calligraphy and traditional ink and wash painting in his home studio. Lee Po Ng is the author's father.

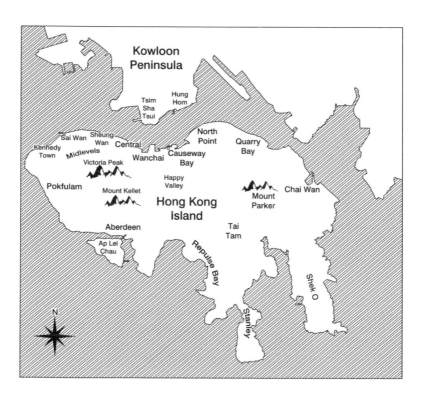

Map of Hong Kong Island

Timeline of Key Events

1839 - 1841	First Opium War between China and Britain
1841	Britain occupies Hong Kong Island
1842	China cedes Hong Kong Island to Britain
1861	Britain occupies Kowloon Peninsula
1894	The bubonic plague strikes Hong Kong
1899	Britain occupies the New Territories
1912	Sun Yat-sen founds the Republic of China
1927 – 1936	Chinese Civil War
1931 – 1945	Japanese invasion of China
1941 – 1945	Japanese occupation of Hong Kong
1946 – 1949	Chinese Civil War continues
1949	Mao Zedong founds the People's Republic of China
1958 – 1961	The Great Leap Forward in China
1966 – 1976	The Cultural Revolution in China
1967	Leftists' Riots in Hong Kong
1984	China and Britain sign the Joint Declaration over the return of Hong Kong
1989	Tiananmen Square Massacre in Beijing
1997	Hong Kong's sovereignty reverts to China
1997 - 1998	The Asian Financial Crisis
2001	China joins the World Trade Organization
2003	The SARS outbreak strikes Hong Kong
2007 - 2008	The Global Financial Tsunami
2011	China becomes the world's second largest economy
2014	The Umbrella Movement erupts with student protesters occupying large swaths of Hong Kong

Part 1
Our Way of Life

Lords and Serfs

I

Feudalism emerged in 8th Century Europe as a social structure to restore stability following the fall of the Roman Empire. For several hundred years, medieval empires were ruled not by central governments but by regional lords. They were powerful landowners who levied their own taxes and dispensed their own justice. On the other end of the social spectrum were the serfs. Bound for life to their lords, they toiled in the fields and relinquished control over every aspect of their disenfranchised existence.

What little we remember from our 8th grade history class has taken on new meaning in land scarce Hong Kong. The combination of overpopulation and business friendly housing policies has given a handful of property developers free rein to multiply their economic power and act like medieval overlords. Meanwhile, the proletariat hunkers down day after grueling day, only to pour their life savings into the bubbling cauldron of the property market. The cost of a 500-square-foot apartment is now 250 times the median monthly household income, a historical high. Homeowners spend on average 57% of their monthly income – over half of their paychecks – on their mortgage payments. Once we tally up how much "housing tax" we pay to the property cartel every year, the city's 15% income tax rate suddenly doesn't seem like such a bargain.

Think of the real estate market in Hong Kong as a high stakes board game for the super rich. As Parker Brothers, maker of *Monopoly*, succinctly put it in the 1936 rule sheet: "The idea of the game is to buy, rent and sell properties so profitably that one becomes the wealthiest player and eventual monopolist." Big property developers have done exactly that. After half a century of rolling the dice and going around the board, Hongkong Land now owns half of Central, Hysan has claimed Causeway Bay, Swire controls Admiralty and Quarry Bay, and Cheung Kong holds Hung Hom, Cyberport and Ap Lei Chau. Together, they have carved up the city and staked out their turf, making Hong Kong the world's largest game board. The analogy is perhaps what inspired MTR Corp., operator of our subway system and now a major property developer, to pick a distinct color for each of its stations.

Selling the same cookie cutter apartments in building after building, however profitable, can get a little dull. Eager to branch out, property developers have mushroomed into colossal conglomerates with tentacles reaching into every corner of our lives. Cheung Kong and Henderson, two of the city's largest developers, own and operate retail chains, utilities, public transport and mobile phone services. Being the landlords of prime retail space has given them an upper hand over their competitors.

Property Developers and Their Reach

Group	Cheung Kong, Hutchison, Whampoa, PCCW	Henderson Land	Sun Hung Kai Properties	Wheelock Properties	New World Development	Jardine Matheson, Hongkong Land	Swire	MTR Corp.
Chairman	Li Ka-shing & sons 李嘉誠父子	Lee Shau-kee 李兆基	Kwok Brothers 郭氏兄弟	Peter Woo 吳光正	Henry Cheng 鄭家純	Sir Henry Keswick	Barnaby Swire	Frederick Ma 馬時亨
Flagship Residential Developments	Whampoa, Bel-Air, South Horizons, City Garden, Kingswood Villas, Laguna City	Grand Promenade, City One, Amoy Gardens, Metro City Plaza, Wonderland Villas	Leighton Hill, Manhattan Hill, YoHo Town, Tai Po Centre, Tsuen Wan Centre	Sorrento, Parc Oasis	Mei Foo, Baguio Villa, Bedford Gardens, Discovery Park	Chi Fu Fa Yuen, Serenade, The Sail at Victoria, Ivy on Belcher's	Tai Koo Shing, Lei King Wan, Yau Yat Tsuen, Beacon Heights, Ocean Shores	Olympian City, Heng Fa Chuen, Telford Gardens, Luk Yeung Sun Chuen, Kornhill
Flagship Commercial Developments	Cyberport, Cheung Kong Centre, Hutchison House	IFC, ICC, Metro City Plaza	IFC, ICC, Langham Place, New Town Plaza	Harbour City, Times Square, Wheelock House	New World Centre, K-11	Landmark, Exchange Square, Jardine House	Taikoo Place, City Plaza, Pacific Place	Telford Plaza, Luk Yeung Galleria, Maritime Square
Retail Chains	Watson's, Fortress	Jusco		Lane Crawford, Joyce	Chow Tai Fook	Mannings		
Food & Dining	Park'n Shop, Watson's Wine, Watson's Water	Miramar Group		City Super		Wellcome, Maxim's Group, Dairy Farm		
Public Transport			Kowloon Motor Bus	Star Ferry	First Bus, First Ferry, City Bus		Cathay Pacific, Dragon Air	MTR, Kowloon-Canton Railway
Utilities	HK Electric, Three, PCCW	Towngas	SmarTone	Cable TV	New World Telecom			
Others	Ports, hotels, biotech	Hotels	Ports	Ports, hotels	Hotels	Hotels, insurance, car dealerships	Hotels	

Source: Hong Kong Stock Exchange filings. Table does not reflect ownership changes since publication.

Their market power is not unlike that of the *zaibatsu* (財閥; literally, financial cliques) in Japan and the *chaebol* in South Korea. The difference between Cheung Kong and Mitsubishi or Samsung is one of degree rather than kind. It is all the more ironic that Hong Kong is ranked the freest economy in the world year after year. But free for whom? Whoever conducts these studies should walk a mile in our shoes and see for themselves how deep the property tycoons' hands are in our pockets.

There is a longstanding assumption that no one can effectively govern Hong Kong without the full cooperation of the property czars. The Chinese leadership went to great lengths to get on their good side during the handover negotiations with Britain in the 1970s and 80s. Today, land sale proceeds, property tax and stamp duty together account for over 40% of the government's total revenue, which has given property developers tremendous sway over policymakers. The alignment of their interests has raised suspicions of a *quid pro quo* relationship between the two. Construction of subsidized public housing, for instance, was halted for a decade between 2003 and 2013 to prop up the prices of private residences. The Competition Act, originally designed to break up the monopolists, was declawed and neutered like a house pet before it was signed into law in 2013. It is little wonder that property tycoons in Hong Kong swagger around town like Al Capone in the 1920s.

Refusing to submit to modern day feudalism, a small group of citizens are waging a resistance movement against the overlords. They partake in their own brand of civil disobedience by boycotting businesses run by the property cartel. These renegades live in old tenement buildings instead of modern towers built by big developers. They buy food from mom-and-pop grocers, bicycle to work and use free Wi-Fi access at public libraries. But their resistance is futile, for even the most defiant of rebels still need electricity to run their homes and mobile service to connect to the outside world. Though their sacrifices are noble, these Don Quixotes have not made the slightest dent in the cartel's windmill.

What's remarkable about this budding social movement, however, is that its warriors are not desperate homebuyers who have been priced out of the property market. Instead, they come from the city's intelligentsia: artists, writers, professors and architects. The rebels are shouting out to the silent majority that property developers have done much more than hijack our economy; rather, they are stifling our creativity, entrepreneurship and other things that make our city great. Sky high retail rent is forcing fashion designers and pastry chefs to think better of their survival and give up their dreams before they see the light of day. Small businesses are uniformly caught in a Catch 22: make too little money and they can't pay rent; make too much, and their rent will quadruple next year. It is this twisted reality, not a lack of talent, that has given Hong Kong the nickname "cultural desert."

Nevertheless, there are signs that the days of the property cartel's dominance are numbered. Almost two decades after the handover, the assumption that Beijing still needs the tycoons to govern the city is increasingly being challenged. In the meantime, China has begun to gradually take over local businesses in Hong Kong. They are bankrolling mainland conglomerates to outbid their Hong Kong counterparts in everything from land to business licenses and 3G bandwidth. Even "Superman" Li Ka-shing, founder and chairman of Cheung Kong, sees the writing on the wall and is pulling his assets out of the city. The changing of the guard, however, is unlikely to make much of a difference to the average citizen. As soon as one empire falls, another one just as formidable will take over.

Li Ka-shing, Chairman of Cheung Kong

In all, the Middle Ages lasted 11 centuries. Before the Renaissance breathed new life into civilization, Europe went through 300 years of famine, plague and social unrest. Historians call it the Dark Ages. If Hong Kongers would take a page from the history books, we can expect our descent into serfdom to get a lot worse before it gets better.

II

Our society is divided into two groups of people: those who own property and those who are trying to.

For years after I left New York City and moved to Hong Kong, my parents would nag me about buying a home. They would tell me to start with something small and slowly work my way up. Renting, to use their words, is like throwing money into the ocean. I would dismiss their advice as platitudes from *The*

Chinese Book of Conventional Wisdom. If such a book did exist, there would be a soaring dragon and cloud motifs on the cover, and the first chapter would be about how property is the only failsafe investment in life.

Apparently my parents aren't the only people who have read the imaginary book. It seems that everyone in Hong Kong has a copy too – for the same line of questioning keeps popping up in every social conversation: *Do you rent or own? Where? How much?* Americans think New Yorkers are property obsessed, but clearly they haven't lived a day in Hong Kong. In this part of the world, a man isn't a man until he is a homeowner. His entire life leads up to the singular moment when he hands over the down-payment check and puts his signature on the triplicate purchase agreement. All the good grades and job promotions he has received are mere preparation; and every source of happiness – marriage, children and retirement – depends on it. I used to find the property culture in Hong Kong unhealthy and borderline insane. It's not how I wanted to live my life.

Then came the financial tsunami in 2008. Property prices in Hong Kong tumbled on the heels of the American housing crisis. My parents' voices were once again ringing in my head: Get in *now* or regret it later! They had a point. Real estate might be one big pyramid scheme, but at some point I had to think about putting a permanent roof over my head. So when my landlady left me a voicemail hinting at a rent increase, it was the straw that broke the renter's back. I decided to hop off my moral high horse and walk boldly into one of the dozen real estate agents in Central. I figured if I couldn't beat the property tycoons, I might as well join them.

Buying property is a quintessential Hong Kong experience. It is as if brokers from agencies like Centaline (中原) and Midland

(美聯) were trained at the same boot camp and taught the same tricks. They all start their clients off by showing them tiny, overpriced units they call "foil listings" (射盤). The idea is to manage expectations and make everything else they show look good by comparison. After that comes the sweet talk. Dodgy neighborhoods are dressed up with euphemisms like "up and coming," "quaint" and, if there's such a word, "enclavish." "Tree view" means the unit is on a low floor and "city view" means it is within handshaking distance from the adjacent building. Playing to the homebuyers' superstition, they often cite pseudo-scientific principles about energy flows and bedroom orientation, and tell them how the unit had brought the previous owner so much luck that he traded up for a duplex in Repulse Bay.

Centaline, one of the largest real estate agencies in Hong Kong

Still, the agents' honey-dripping tongues pale in comparison to the property developers' sleight of hand. Industry tricks to squeeze every penny from homebuyers range from employing optical illusions to exploiting legal loopholes. For instance, miniature furniture and paper thin walls are used in model homes to make the unit appear bigger and more livable. To maximize the gross floor area (GFA) permitted under the government land lease, developers sacrifice functionality for profit and come up with strangely shaped living rooms, stamp-sized balconies and other "only in Hong Kong" layouts. Unnecessary features like bay windows and public green areas are supersized because building regulations exclude them from the GFA calculation. As a result, homebuyers end up paying an extra 30% to 40% for space they don't want and can't really use. Despite the ornate lobbies and fancy club houses, behind the apartment door is just another typical Hong Kong shoebox where the flat screen TV stands three feet from the sofa and where the barred windows look straight into someone else's living room.

Refusing to be gouged by property developers, I told the agents to focus on pre-owned, postwar buildings in Sheung Wan and SoHo. I must have viewed a hundred listings over the course of a few weeks. Though the idea of living in an old walkup sounded romantic in my head, in reality many of these units were too run-down to justify the multi-million dollar investment. Just when I was about to give up, I stumbled into my dream home in a 45-year-old building in Pokfulam, a quiet neighborhood on the southside of the island. Part euphoric and part home shopping fatigued, I signed the papers the following day.

Everything after that happened very quickly. The process of ownership transfer is so streamlined in Hong Kong that it feels almost casual. I had expected more pomp and circumstance, or at least a simple handshake. The sanctity of property investment seems to have been lost in the shuffle because lawyers and mortgage loan officers deal with thousands of transactions like mine every month. What remains, on the other hand, is a handful of bizarre practices. For instance, my agent told me there was one minor check to perform before the scheduled closing. He needed to vet the apartment against the "haunted house list" on the Internet. All clear, he declared after tapping on his iPad, no one was murdered or committed suicide in my new home. I thanked him and handed him the commission check.

It took nearly four months for my contractor to have the unit gutted and renovated to my liking. The moment I turned the key and walked into the empty flat still reeking of fresh paint, I felt more grown up than I had ever felt before. The sense of ownership was overwhelming – it was as if every brick and tile had my name on it. Never again would I be at the mercy of greedy landlords who would raise my rent every two years or kick me out when a better tenant came along. I could change the color of the walls and hang things on them without losing my security deposit. I finally understood why, despite all the resentment toward the property tycoons, citizens still willingly put on the shackles of a mortgage and become indentured servants. There is no price too high for home ownership.

Since I purchased my apartment four years ago, its value has nearly doubled. It sounds impressive but it is all just a paper gain. If I were to take profit by selling my home, every dollar I made would have to be plowed right back into the market for a replacement property. It would be a complete wash, even if I discount all the stamp duty, agent's commissions, lawyers' fees and the cost of another lengthy renovation.

For now I am content with what I have. More so, I am grateful for my parents' advice. If I had waited any longer, I would have been in the same position as so many others who are praying every day for another market crash, like the ones we witnessed in 1998, 2003 and 2008. Their bad wishes are motivated not by malice but by necessity, for the elusive goal of home ownership is putting their life plans indefinitely on hold. It is an unenviable situation from which I narrowly escaped. As much as I hate to admit it, when it comes to money matters, conventional Chinese wisdom does have the last word.

No City for Slow Men

I

You, out of my way! All you people who walk at a glacial pace, who pause in front of the subway turnstiles searching for your Octopus cards: step aside and move over! And all you waiters, drycleaners and Starbucks coffee boys: hurry, pronto, chop chop! I don't have all day!!

He might have to skip lunch again

That isn't the rant of a Canto-pop diva on a bad hair day; it is the collective stream of consciousness of the seven million citizens who move like characters in an over-cranked silent film. Hong Kong is a city in perpetual motion. We cover our streets with escalators and travelators to take us up, down and across. We bulldoze onto the train before others get off and we bulldoze off the plane as soon as it touches the tarmac. At a shopping mall in Causeway Bay, the walking times from the lobby to the parking lot are posted on the walls: 55 seconds to Level B4; 80 seconds to Level B5. Keeping time in hours and minutes is so last century.

Speed is in our DNA. What Hong Kongers and the 13 species of Darwin's finches have in common is that both have evolved spectacularly to adapt to their habitats. Whereas the exotic birds have developed highly specialized beaks, we have mutated into serial multi-taskers. Natural selection has caused taxi drivers to mount a dozen cell phones on their dashboards and carry on multiple conversations while negotiating the urban maze. At any noodle house during the lunch hour, staff take orders, serve food, squash bugs and place bets on horse races in perfectly choreographed movements like a ballet company performing *Flight of the Bumblebee*. We are genetically programmed to feel unproductive unless we are doing at least three things at once.

Then there are the slow people – how we loathe the slow people! In supersonic Hong Kong, they get pushed aside and ridiculed. Cantonese is a colorful language and we lavish the paint on the evolutionary outcast. In the local vernacular, they "crawl like ants" and "keep the world from spinning." I once heard a street vendor describe two laid back Filipino helpers as "having eaten ten barrels of pig fat." Indeed, foreigners accustomed to their *joie de vivre* and *dolce vita* often bear the brunt of our ire. We balk at lost tourists who meander and reverse direction on the sidewalk and clueless expats who ask too many questions at a dim sum restaurant. What these people don't know – and what we simply don't have the time to explain to them – is that Hong Kong is no place to stop and smell the roses. The only thing we put our noses to is the grindstone. Forgive us if we seem crass, but we have a 14-hour day ahead of us and a 30-year mortgage to pay off.

In our 24-hour city, "time is money" is more than a cliché. According to research by American sociologist Robert Levine, there is a strong correlation between a city's pace of life and its affluence. Whereas places with active economies put greater value on time, those that value time are also more likely to have active economies. The causality between tempo and wealth goes both ways and the two variables form a positive feedback loop. That's a fancy way of saying that it pays to be in a hurry, a lesson that the local population has taken to heart. To a teacher who moonlights as a real estate broker, the opportunity cost of going straight home after school makes it a very expensive proposition.

Nevertheless, Levine's research also links a fast pace of life to stress-related ailments like coronary heart disease. In Hong Kong, our obsession with speed has led to a high incidence of indigestion and anxiety. While citizens point their fingers at a punishing work culture, in reality much of the pain is self-inflicted. Hong Kongers have a propensity to over-promise and under-deliver. We believe we can make up for lost time, sometimes even *create* time, by working harder and smarter. That's why we agree to finish a job in two days when we know it will take a week. "On our way" means we are about to jump out of bed and into the shower. The more we try to impress, the more we disappoint others and corner ourselves. The positive feedback loop can easily turn into a vicious circle of stress and haste.

I am guilty of all of the above. I spread myself too thin and take on more than I can chew. As a freelance writer I never turn down a call for contributions, and as a friend I double, sometimes triple, book my weekends. I power walk like an Olympian even when I am not in a rush. I once took a "leisurely" evening stroll along the scenic perimeter of Hangzhou's famous West Lake and found myself racing at 10 kilometers an hour. My mother always tells me my strings are strung too tight. She warns me they may snap one day.

The strings do snap once in a while. Getting the seasonal flu is my body's way of calling a time out. For days I will be bedridden and unable to do anything but sleep. Every now and then, a minor injury at the gym – straining a muscle or spraining an ankle – will make me limp for weeks and appreciate what it's like to live on the other end of the speed continuum. Pedestrians will swoosh past me and elevator doors will close in my face. Buses will take off and leave me in the dust while I hobble my way to the stop. To be a slow man in a fast city is to be a rock in the middle of the raging river – to be awash with the feeling of being left behind, unwanted and irrelevant.

When we were children, we were told the merits of hard work. "The early bird gets the worm," we were told, and "you snooze you lose." We read *The Tortoise and the Hare* and learned the dire consequences of taking even a short break. So we stuff our calendar like a Thanksgiving turkey and wring every ounce of use out of our day. Nevertheless, as simple pleasures in life, like sitting down for a proper meal or watching our children grow up, continue to elude us, more and more people are waking up to the perils of rushing through life. We fear that on our deathbeds we will remember not birthday candles or footprints on the beach, but pay slips and bank statements. Success, we realize, should be measured in bike rides and sunsets instead of tick marks and dollar signs. In 21st Century Hong Kong, Aesop's famous fable needs a rewrite – both the tortoise and the hare need to smell some roses and take a nap together.

II

World Sauntering Day is a little known holiday celebrated every 19 June as a reminder that we should take a breather and appreciate what's around us. The world is our oyster and for at least one day a year we ought to savor it unhurriedly.

The holiday has been slow to catch on. For one thing, the idea of celebrating leisure in 24 hours is somewhat self-defeating. For another, there are more regular and effective ways to de-stress. Every culture has its preferred way to go about it: the Japanese have their onsens and the Indians have yoga. The Russians drink vodka and play the balalaika. However, it is the French who have perfected the art of slowing down. A day in the republic is not complete without a cup of coffee after a long lunch, a cigarette break at 4pm and an evening of *cuisine à domicile* with wine and more coffee and cigarettes.

Humming her stress away

People in Hong Kong face a particular challenge when we try to unwind: a lack of square footage. To borrow Irish statesman Edmund Burke's famous words, "Our repose is troubled and our pleasures are saddened" – in our case, not by the French Revolution but by the lack of space and privacy at home. Putting on music annoys older folks and lighting candles is too much of a fire hazard. Taking a bubble bath means putting our face inches from the toilet bowl. That is, if no one else is using the toilet and if there is room for a tub in the first place!

But we can't blame it all on the lack of space. Hong Kong is a highly regimented city: movies on Friday nights and dim sum brunches every Sunday morning. We go hiking when it is sunny, and hit the mall when it rains. Herd mentality is the reason why we constantly run into each other in the same places. Worse, we are pathological trend chasers – if it isn't the newest and the latest, it just isn't worth our time. Hipsters and wannabes mob the same new restaurants, new stores and even new hospitals. Not even standing in a 50-person deep line will deter the lemmings from jumping off the cliff.

The same observation can be made for our holidays. I never understand why the entire city must descend on the cemeteries on Ching Ming (清明節; Tomb Sweeping Day) or why we let florists and restaurants gouge us every Valentine's Day. Surely our dead relatives wouldn't mind getting a visit on their birthdays instead, and wouldn't our spouses prefer a better gift on 15 February? None of that seems to register. The bandwagon hurtles on, and baffled riders wonder why the cabin has no space.

Instead of an annual World Sauntering Day, I propose a Do Something Different Day. It's a festival we can celebrate every weekend. Going off the beaten path is the only sure way to slow down on our own terms. Here are a few simple ideas anyone can

39

try: read a book at a quaint café, visit a deserted neighborhood with a good quality camera, or watch a sunset on the Sheung Wan waterfront. Not radical enough? Head to the beach when it rains and watch raindrops dance on the ocean surface. Go hiking at night with a flashlight and listen to the crickets sing. Find a patch of green in a country park, spread open a straw mat and savor soft cheese with a bottle of wine. The idea is to break away from the pack and swim against the tide.

Thinking outside the box is easier said than done, especially in conformist Hong Kong. None of these ideas makes for glamorous Facebook posts. Some of them may even elicit worried looks from friends and family. Sometimes the plans aren't executed well and may feel like, God forbid, a waste of time. Every now and then, however, we stumble upon something that works and we hold on to it like Linus to his blanket. Knowing that we have options can be very liberating in itself.

*   *   *

They say anyone can see a sunset, but we have to work for a sunrise. Taking the old adage to heart, I woke up at 5am yesterday and walked up the hiking trail near my home. I arrived at the Peak just as pale golden lights streamed between the hills. Summer breezes rustled through the woods bringing the leafy scent of dew. A dragonfly hovered. A host of sparrows chirped in lazy intermittence. Nothing around me offered the slightest inkling that the ant colony down below was about to wake up to another boisterous day.

Hong Kong is charming when it is bustling, but loveliest when it is tranquil. The city's placid side is there for the taking, if only we look hard enough. The same can be said about its people. Our gentler, more tempered nature needs to be nurtured with patience. Surviving in a big city can be like approaching a beehive: sometimes the best way to do it is to slow down.

Horo-Logic

Ernest and I have been friends for over 25 years. I was the best man at his wedding and I am his baby daughter's godfather. An engineer by trade, Ernest designs websites for a living. While his freelance business can be choppy, he always manages to keep an even keel. He pays his mortgage, feeds his family and takes them on a vacation once a year.

I meet Ernest for drinks almost every month. We were at a bar on Wyndham Street last week when he said he wanted my opinion on something. It sounded serious – I thought his wife Rosalyn was pregnant again. A second child would put a strain on his finances.

"I am thinking of getting a watch," Ernst announced.

The tone of his voice suggested that he didn't mean a Casio. "You mean... like a Rolex?" I ventured a guess. He nodded, ready to be judged.

Ernest is not into brands or flashy things. He scoffs at people who wear Gucci shoes and carry Louis Vuitton bags. Hong Kong is a materialistic place and he is one of the last low maintenance men standing. This is not a person to drop three months' income on a piece of man jewelry.

"Why all of a sudden?" I refrained from judgment.

"It's for my business. You know how it is."

Of course I did. I also knew what button to press and I went for it. "What did Rosalyn say?"

"I haven't told her yet."

*   *   *

Hong Kong boasts the world's highest per capita consumption of "extra old" cognac, better known as "X.O." Our thirst for expensive liquor is matched only by our appetite for high end watches. More Rolexes are sold on this speck of land than any country on the entire planet. The remarkable statistic is due in large part to the constant influx of well-heeled mainland Chinese tourists in search of authentic, tax free luxury goods. Their retail blitzes have transformed popular shopping areas like Causeway Bay and Tsim Sha Tsui into the World Expo for horology. Russell Street, Hennessey Road and Canton Road are lined back-to-back with Cartier, Omega, Piaget and, of course, Rolex stores. The nearest restaurant is several blocks away or up an office building. Even clothing boutiques and shoe stores are being displaced to make room for more bling. They say variety is the spice of life, but don't tell that to the landlords who can raise the rent several times by leasing only to the *Grandes Maisons*. After all, how many thousand bowls of wonton soups does a noodle house have to sell to match the margin of an 18-carat rose gold Rolex Daytona?

Man's best friend

Hong Kong's longstanding love affair with watches predates the arrival of mainland tourists. In my father's generation, owning a *gum lo* (金勞; the Cantonese slang for a gold Rolex) was not only a status symbol; it was also a ready line of credit. Back then, a man would rush to the pawn shop at the first sign of financial trouble and turn in his timekeeper for cash. Once the crisis had subsided, he would redeem the collateral and click it back on his wrist. Order would be restored and both man and machine would be as good as new.

A generation later, the city is more affluent and pawn shops are all but extinct. Though time has changed, our devotion to Swiss movement hasn't. My expat friends are constantly amazed by the way men in Hong Kong spend more on watches than what folks back home do on sports cars. They are also befuddled by how commonplace these watches are. A managing director at an investment bank may make 30 times the salary of an entry level analyst, but the two men may easily be wearing the same HK$80,000 (US$10,000) timepiece. It is as indispensable to men as Coco Chanel's 2.55 handbag is to the battalion of "office ladies" in Central. It is a Hong Kong thing.

Whenever men need an excuse to buy an expensive watch, they will invariably invoke the "i" word: investment. It is the same argument men use to justify spending obscene amounts on artwork and vintage wines. They can call it what they may, but a purchase is only an investment if the owners are willing to part with it. People looking to drop serious cash on a piece of metal, as my friend Ernest did, aren't thinking of ever selling it. Even if they are, watches are not a particularly good investment. Contrary to popular belief, they almost never go up in value. A brand new timepiece depreciates by 20% the moment you take it out of the store. Whoever thinks he can buy a Rolex, wear it for a few years and sell it at a profit is fooling himself – and his wife.

Once the investment argument is debunked, men turn to the age old sales pitch uttered at used car dealerships and real estate offices across the city: buy now or risk paying more later. It operates on the assumption that every self-respecting man must own a luxury watch at some point in their lives. Since you are going to buy one sooner or later, says the snake oil salesman, why not lock in the price now and enjoy the awesomeness right away? The logic is not only infallible, it is also borne out by empirical evidence. In the past decade, the exponential growth in watch sales has allowed big brands to revise their price lists every few months. Earlier this year, my brother Kelvin was looking to buy a Cartier Ballon Bleu. During the six months he took to mull over the decision, the price went up by 15%. My brother's prudent deliberation turned out to be very imprudent.

If Kelvin's story is not enough to make you rush out to the Rolex store, then consider another rationale. To be taken seriously in Hong Kong, you need to not just look the part but be visibly successful. It is especially true in client-facing industries where prosperity is often one's only source of credibility. After all, no one wants to hire a financial planner who doesn't manage his own money well enough to afford nice things. Among all the things we can throw on our bodies to signal success, the watch is the most noticeable, durable and universally understood. It is wearable wealth in its purest form, cloaked under a thin veneer of utility: Swiss workmanship, 100-meter water resistance and accuracy to the hundredth of a second – as if we were all divers and nuclear physicists.

Owning an expensive watch is a lot like having a girlfriend – it is not a big deal to have one, but it is a big deal *not* to. In Hong Kong, you often catch the person talking to you sizing you up like a full body scanner at JFK Airport. His eyes will stay on your wrist just long enough for him to zero in on the brand and price range. As a freelancer who needs to meet new clients on a regular basis, Ernest is constantly subject to the appraising eye of his prospective customers. A watch has become as much a part of his credentials as his CV and portfolio. That's what Ernest meant when he uttered those sobering words: *You know how it is.*

*   *   *

Three weeks after our drinks on Wyndham Street, Ernest took the plunge. After invoking all the logic a man can summon to justify the purchase, he finally got Rosalyn's blessing. He contacted a friend of a friend who knew an assistant manager at King Fook, one of the largest watch retailers in the city, and got him to shave 8% off the ticket price. That's the way to do it, because here in Hong Kong, everyone knows someone in the watch business and no one ever pays the walk-in price. A Rolex GMT Submariner with a black ceramic bezel now adorns my friend's previously barren wrist. He is a happy man.

"Perhaps it's all in my head, but I sound more confident at meetings these days," Ernest said, quite aware of the irony of having become someone he used to poke fun at. My friend may have gained confidence and some new business, but he has lost something too – the moral authority to scoff at people who wear Gucci shoes and carry Louis Vuitton bags. Another low maintenance man bites the dust.

More Pet Peeves

Five years ago I wrote an essay about my pet peeves. For those who are unfamiliar with the expression, a pet peeve is a minor annoyance in life that drives you up the wall but you don't quite understand why. You can literally feel your blood pressure rise when, for instance, someone keeps talking during a movie or misuses the word "literally" – as I just did to show you how annoying that can be.

Some of these small offenses are universally loathed, like the two examples I have just raised. Others, however, are genetically engineered to bother you and only you. They make your skin crawl but people around you will barely even notice them. You ask yourself, "Is it just me?" and the answer is invariably "Duh."

I decided to write a Part 2 for two reasons. First, it turns out that I am not the only neurotic nutcase around here. Part 1 has been vindicated by readers who told me they too share the same sentiment. One of them had this to say during a recent book club discussion: "I know it's not nice to complain about babies, but airlines should put a time limit on how long they are permitted to cry before someone shoots them with an elephant tranquilizer!" Out of control children was number 4 on my list.

Second, and more disturbingly, my pet peeves have been growing like a magical beanstalk. I opened Pandora's Box and out came the nose picker, the soup slurper, the loud talker, the close talker and the slow talker. Perhaps time has made me a grouch. Or perhaps the world has become more intolerable since Michael Jackson died and Michael Douglas filed for divorce. Whatever it is, here is another top ten list of my personal pet peeves that are, once again, obsessive compulsively arranged in order of increasing annoyance.

1. The Arctic Blast – In Hong Kong, nothing says luxury like bone chilling indoor temperature. It is as if the class of a shopping mall is measured by the horsepower of its air-conditioners. This misguided retail philosophy has been applied to public transport, the gym and the office, forcing citizens to wear sweaters and shawls even during the dog days of summer. And for what? Just so Dior and Gucci can offload their winter coats and shoppers have an excuse to show them off.

2. Foreign Names – Plenty of ink has been spilled on the weird names Hong Kongers give themselves. Every day we run into respectable people called Devil, Mistress and Nitrogen. Funny names are amusing, but not irritating. What crosses the line is when Chinese people start using Japanese, Italian or French names. The city is now filled with girls called Suki and Yuko and guys named Giovanni and Jacques (instead of John and Jack). We adopt Anglo-Saxon names because Hong Kong is a former British colony and because English is the *lingua franca* in the business world and on the Internet. I am sorry, but Giuseppe Chan just sounds ridiculous. So if John and Jane are too boring, then please just stick to Creamy and Chlorophyll.

3. PDA – The acronym normally stands for "public display of affection." It refers to people who French kiss in a restaurant or make out in the movie theater. In Hong Kong, however, it stands for "public display of annoyance." I am talking about people who huff and puff when they miss an elevator, tap their shoes loudly in the checkout line or roll their eyes with a slow cashier. Then there are couples who get into explosive fights in public, which, despite popular belief that Asian people are conscious of face, is a rather common sight in Hong Kong. PDA sucks up all the positive energy within a 15-feet radius and is the last thing this stressful city needs.

4. The Lone English Speaker – There is a subset of Western expats living in Hong Kong who think that they are the only English speaking people around. They believe that all Chinese people must sound like Jackie Chan in a kung fu comedy. One time at H&M, a white store manager with a thick Aussie accent said to me, "My colleague told me you were looking for this T-shirt in blue...Oh sorry, do you speak English?" The last four words were uttered in slow motion, complete with hand gestures. I promptly hit back with "I do. But do you?" And to any *gweilo* who patronizes us with the dubious compliment "Wow, you speak very good English," our standard answer should be: "Wow, so do you!"

5. *The Public Groomer* – I am sitting quietly on the minibus when I hear "click, click, click" from across the aisle. I frantically check for shrapnel and sure enough, an ivory-colored crescent with a black lining has landed right on my left thigh. Nail clipping in public is not only disgusting, but also downright dangerous, especially when performed on a minibus going 80 kilometers an hour. The same goes for beauty conscious "office ladies" who apply eyeliner on a swerving vehicle. I may not know anything about makeup, but I'm pretty sure that having a pencil stuck in a bloody eyeball is not considered attractive.

The gentleman on the right forgot his earphones

6. *The Broadcaster* – As if we don't already have enough people talking loudly in public, there is now a new breed of technorati who prefer to watch movies or play video games on public transport without earphones. Either they find those earbuds too snug for comfort or they have forgotten them at home. Or they are just really keen on sharing their funny YouTube videos. I never hesitate to tap them on the shoulder and tell them to turn the sound off, which on occasion has earned me cheers and applause from the silent sufferers near me.

7. *The Nosy Rosy* – "Do you have a girlfriend?" "Do you rent or own your apartment?" "Where did you get those jeans?" The interrogator is not my mom or even a nosy relative. She is the security guard who works at my dentist's building. Unless this person moonlights as a matchmaker or is an undercover statistician for Hong Kong University, there is no good reason for her curiosity. Most likely she is just bored, which is why she goes on to say, "Nice watch! Is it expensive?"

8. *The Road Block*. Newton's first law of motion stipulates that when a family of four walk on a crowded street in Hong Kong, they must do so shoulder-to-shoulder, hand-in-hand like a curtain call at the Royal Shakespeare Theatre. The second law requires pedestrians to linger at the landing of an escalator while they ponder where to go next. The third one, as every high school student can regurgitate, is action and reaction. My standard reaction is to say "SCUSE ME!" before breaching the human wall like Moses parting the Red Sea.

9. *The Taxi Thief* – The rain is coming down in sheets and I have been standing by the curb waiting for a taxi for a good 15 minutes. Some guy comes out of a building, sees me and walks 10 steps in front of me. I would respond in kind if I wasn't carrying a heavy load of groceries while struggling to keep the umbrella upright. I also don't want to stoop to his level. I remember an expat friend once observed that there are two types of people in Hong Kong: selfish and very selfish. I start to believe him and question my faith in humanity. I wonder whether the raindrops are actually angel tears.

10. *The Self-regulator* – Former Governor of Hong Kong Chris Patten famously said that our autonomy wouldn't be taken away by Beijing. Instead, it would be given away bit by bit by people in Hong Kong in exchange for personal gain. Patten's foresight is also applicable to the dynamics between management and staff in the workplace. In Hong Kong, self-regulation is our way of sucking up to those in high position. It is not uncommon to hear things like: "We shouldn't eat Chinese food in the pantry, the boss doesn't like the smell," or "'Let's not bring up flexible hours at the department meeting, *lo ban* doesn't want to hear it." So bit by bit, these people voluntarily hand over their rights, the same way some of our politicians do with our freedoms. The sad thing is that *lo ban* – or Beijing for that matter – doesn't even have to ask.

*   *   *

Nowadays, whenever I am about to lose my cool over a pet peeve, I will take a deep breath and look up at the sky. I try to remember the 12-step anger management program I never attended and probably should. Still, every time I hear people talk during a movie, I will instinctively reach into my bag searching for the hand grenade I don't have but wish I did.

購物不如淘寶

Why Shop When You Can Taobao?

Imagine you wanted to show up at work every day carrying a different Hermès handbag. Imagine you had a six-month-old baby at home who was in constant need of diapers and baby formula. And imagine you had just bought a new apartment and you needed to furnish the whole place from living room to kitchen. Don't go looking at the Landmark, Watson's, or IKEA, because retail shopping is so 2007. Instead, you can stay right at home and start treasure hunting online at Taobao (淘寶), the world's biggest marketplace. It is Shopping 3.0.

Taobao is the Internet's best kept secret. The site, which literally means searching for treasures in Mandarin, is a combination of Amazon and eBay. It is increasingly the first place Chinese shoppers look to for clothing, cosmetics and everyday household supplies. If you can type it in Chinese, they will sell it. Some of the strangest items sold include pet pigs, Botox injections and breast milk. It is Walmart if you could chat with its sales staff at 1am. It is Louis Vuitton if they sold wallets at ¥250 a pop and delivered them right to your doorstep.

Just a few years ago, not many in Hong Kong would admit to shopping at Taobao. Back then, the site with the distinctly mainland-sounding name was synonymous with fakes and knockoffs. But times have changed. Today, Taobao boasts half a billion registered users, nearly twice the United States population. Last year, the site logged ¥1 trillion (US$160 billion) in gross merchandise volume, or total value of goods sold. On every 11 November – China's "Singles' Day" and the biggest online shopping day of the year – the unattached celebrate their singlehood by spending tens of billions of dollars on Taobao purchases in, well, a single day.

With over 800 million product listings, what was once Jack Ma's (Chairman and CEO of Alibaba Group) pet project now makes up over 70% of the entire e-tail market in China. There are blogs and even weekly magazines devoted to helping Taobao fans shop online. Just like Facebook has changed the way we make friends and Apple has revolutionized consumer electronics, Taobao has altered how Chinese people shop. There is no turning back.

So how does it all work? To shop on Taobao, you must be able to read the language, as all the listings are in simplified Chinese. Users can exchange text messages in real time with a salesperson using Ali Wang Wang (阿里旺旺), the site's instant messaging system. This allows shoppers to ask questions about stock availability and delivery charges, and to get instant responses at virtually any time of the day. If you happen to speak Mandarin, you can even talk to a real person. Unlike eBay, Amazon or other online marketplaces, Taobao encourages sellers to publish their telephone numbers and most of them do, making online shopping more personal and interactive than ever.

When you are ready to check out, you pay through Alipay (支付寶), the Chinese version of Paypal. Users can top up their Alipay account using a credit card. Alternatively, shoppers can purchase Taobao credits at any convenience store the same way we refill our Octopus card.

Chairman Ma is the Chinese Jeff Bezos

Shopping on Taobao is not all fun and games. A near universal complaint among shoppers is its user unfriendliness. For Mac users, you either will not find all the necessary plug-ins to complete a purchase or you will spend weeks looking for them. PC users are not immune either – they frequently find the site clunky and hard to navigate. Multiple usernames and passwords are required to traverse between Taobao Marketplace, Alipay and Taodot (淘點), where you deposit your convenience store credit into your account. All that makes Taobao look more like a work in progress than the David who booted Goliath eBay out of China in 2006.

Another common frustration shared by online shoppers is the uncertainty. Shopping on Taobao feels a bit like online dating – the person who shows up at Starbucks rarely looks anything like the profile picture on Match.com. That means if you are determined to find that perfect evening dress for your anniversary dinner on Taobao, it might take you several exchanges before getting what you want. Recognizing that trust is key for e-shopping, Taobao follows eBay's feedback model and allows sellers and buyers to review each other. As a result, most merchants are on their best behavior when it comes to exchanges and refunds. Nevertheless, because things sold on Taobao are much cheaper than at the store, shoppers tend not to bother with returns and end up shoving the purchases in the bottom drawer of the closet.

Over a decade since its inception, Taobao has spawned a new crop of entrepreneurs on the mainland. From college students to desk job haters, China's next generation of millionaires scour factories and wholesale markets for anything sellable and slap a price tag on it. They turn their dorm rooms and living rooms into warehouses and hire photogenic friends to model the goods. Because Taobao does not charge any listing fee or sales commission (the site's revenue comes solely from advertising), sellers get to keep every dollar they make and use it to buy more merchandise and generate more sales. Thanks to courier services like Shun Feng (順豐) – China's answer to UPS and FedEx – shipping charges are as low as a few renminbi for most packages. The Taobao revolution is the reason why the ripping sound of packing tape is echoing around campuses and villages all over China.

At the same time Taobao is fuelling the growth of China's Millionaire Club, it is also improving the quality of life for ordinary citizens. Outside top tier cities like Shanghai and Beijing, the general Chinese population is hardly spoiled for choice when it comes to consumer goods. With Taobao just a mouse click away, however, villagers in remote locations now have access to the same quality products as do folks in Shenzhen or Hong Kong. Recently, a Taiwanese-American friend of mine working in Dalian (大连), a second-tier city in northeast China, wanted to make cupcakes for her children. She quickly discovered that common Western items such as muffin trays and chocolate chips are foreign concepts in most parts of China and that it would have taken her weeks to find the items, if she could find them at all. She did a 10-second search on Taobao and received an entire baking kit the next day.

Two weeks ago, the company I work for upgraded my Blackberry. The new model didn't come with a charging dock. "Not every accessory is available in Hong Kong," the IT guy shrugged. I went on the Internet and found the dock selling at Amazon.com for US$15 (HK$120), but shipping and handling cost another US$50 (HK$400). So where did I look next? You guessed it. With the help of a Taobao savvy friend and for all of ¥20 (US$3), the order arrived at my office two days later in a padded envelope. I now understand why all those Taobao addicts spend nights slouching over their keyboard and filling their living room with things they don't need. Despite popular belief and its rogue status on the U.S. Government's "notorious markets list," Taobao is so much more than just fakes and knockoffs. With hundreds of millions of users turning to it daily for convenience, selections and incredible savings, the site is as much an e-commerce phenomenon as it is a change agent for Chinese society. It won't be long before a new verb enters the English language: taobao with a lowercase "t."

Jack Chang contributed research.

No City for Old Men

I

It is hard to be poor; but it is harder to be poor *and* old. Harder still it is to be so in Hong Kong, a do-it-yourself, get-up-and-go society that would have made Margaret Thatcher salivate. Behind the breathtaking skyline and soaring glass towers, the crisscrossing subway lines and the gravity defying stock market, are hundreds of thousands who go to bed hungry every night.

There are an estimated 1.3 million people living beneath the poverty line in Hong Kong, of which over 300,000 are senior citizens. That number puts one in three elderly people in financial straits. The situation is about to get much worse, as falling birth rates and rising life expectancies are making the city one of the fastest aging populations in the world. By 2040, a mere generation away, people aged 65 or above are expected to account for nearly 30% of Hong Kong's population, up from 13% today. Elderly poverty is a ticking time bomb that, if not defused carefully, will not only threaten the city's long term viability, but also plunge it into an urban humanitarian crisis.

Hong Kong is a self-reliant society. There is a longstanding notion that taxpayers' money should be invested in the productive segment of the population rather than wasting it on the old. Income redistribution is not our cup of tea; eat what you kill is more our thing. It wasn't that long ago when the idea of a public pension system was viewed as an import from the West, a socialist heresy that conjured up images of national debt and sovereign bankruptcies. That's why to most Hong Kongers, the word "pension" was synonymous only with personal savings. Nevertheless, as the city grew more affluent, our understanding of social justice began to shift. So did our expectations of how much our policymakers should try to do.

And tried they have. In 2000, the government implemented a compulsory saving scheme called the Mandatory Provident Fund (MPF) to force citizens to plan for their own retirement. Modeled after the 401(k) in the United States, the scheme requires zero input from the public coffers, which serves our Scrooge-like bureaucrats just fine. With the monthly contribution amount capped at a meager HK$1,250 (US$160), participants are not putting away nearly enough for their retirement. In fact, most people don't bother checking their annual statements because the balance bears so little relevance to the cost of living. What's more, housewives, the unemployed and people making less than HK$6,500 (US$830) a month – the very demographics that need retirement protection the most – are exempted from making a contribution and are therefore left out in the cold. Critics lambaste the scheme as part lip service to social advocacy groups and part handout to big banks that rake in billions in management fees every year. As far as social security policy goes, MPF has been a colossal pork barrel scam.

For millions of households living from paycheck to paycheck, personal savings – through MPF or otherwise – are not an option. They are left with only two lifelines: family support and government assistance.

In traditional Chinese society, the notion of filial piety compels sons and daughters to support their aging parents. Tradition often caves in to reality, however, as many are unable or unwilling to fulfill this non-binding, though no less burdensome, family duty. Then there are retirees who are childless or whose children have moved abroad, in many cases to mainland China for better job prospects. According to the latest government census, the number of elderly citizens who live on their own has jumped 40% in the past decade to 200,000, or one fifth of the senior population. The troubling statistic suggests that children are not as reliable a retirement plan as they once were.

When the first lifeline fails, impoverished elderly turn to their government for help, but with mixed results. In Hong Kong, public assistance takes the form of an old age allowance and social security. Seniors can apply for one or the other but not both.

Old age allowance covers people aged 65 and above. It is commonly known as "fruit money" (生果金) because the amount is so pitifully small: less than HK$1,200 (US$150) a month. That's roughly how much an average household spends on electricity during a summer month. Even the government is embarrassed to call it anything but a "token of respect" for the elderly.

Social security, on the other hand, starts at age 60 and offers assistance of roughly HK$3,000 (US$380) a month. Seniors who live on their own are eligible for an additional housing allowance of around HK$1,500 (US$190) a month. The actual amounts are determined on a case by case basis, but sufficed to say that they are peanuts compared to the actual cost of living in Hong Kong. Moreover, applicants must meet both asset and income tests, which put many of them in a tight spot. For instance, it is a Chinese tradition for the elderly to set aside a modest sum in the bank to cover their own funeral and burial expenses. This so-called "coffin fund" can easily put them over the ludicrously low ceiling of HK$40,000 (US$5,000) under the asset test.

Just as unforgiving, the income test is computed on a household basis instead of an individual basis. To qualify for assistance, applicants living with their working children must either move out or ask them to sign a piece of paper – dubbed the "bad son statement" – certifying that they have cut off the parents from any financial support. All that has led to one result: many eligible seniors would rather struggle on their own than go through the trouble and humiliation to apply for social security.

When both family support and government assistance fail to catch their fall, the elderly are left to fend for themselves. That's why across the city, men and women well into their 60s can be found taking odd jobs: washing dishes in restaurant kitchens or delivering takeout orders to office buildings. The majority who can't find work must take part in Hong Kong's most notorious roadside attraction: the urban scavenger hunt. Every day we see wiry seniors put down their pride and pick up soda cans and plastic bottles from garbage bins. On a good day, they can fetch up to HK$30 (US$4), which, to someone making a subsistence living, can mean two days of groceries – or a shot of insulin.

She has no plan to retire

Aging itself is not scary, what is scary is how unwilling our city is to lend a hand. Calls for a universal pension system have been heard in town hall meetings and the legislature for decades. Countless proposals have been floated by economists, advocacy groups and government taskforces. Despite sitting on HK$800 billion (US$100 billion) in foreign reserves and splurging much of it on wasteful infrastructure projects like the high speed rail link to Shenzhen, our government continues to show little interest in loosening its purse strings to help the elderly. Hong Kong is now shamefully behind neighboring economies like Taiwan and Singapore in providing meaningful social security. Years after we finally play catch up and put in place a comprehensive pension plan, we will look back, just as we did with the minimum wage legislation, and ask why we waited so long.

II

My parents visit Hong Kong once every couple of years. Flying for 16 hours from Toronto is physically demanding for anyone, let alone a septuagenarian couple. My dad doesn't enjoy these trips much because he finds the city claustrophobic. His left leg also gives him trouble with the many stairs and uneven sidewalks. My mom, on the other hand, takes issues with the stifling heat. But seeing her grandchildren makes it all worthwhile. She insists on bringing candies and toys from Canada and passing them around like Mrs. Claus.

During their last visit, my older brother Kelvin and I took them out for dinner at their favorite Chinese restaurant in Wanchai. It was our small way to make up for missing Mother's Days, Father's Days, Christmases and birthdays year after year. We are a typical long distance family – the line between filial piety and guilt is as blurry as my father's eyesight without his bifocals.

After we finished our food, the manager signaled the busboy over to clear our table. The "busboy" was a diminutive woman in her late sixties, her hair grizzled and her back hunched over like a single-hump camel. One by one, she picked up the bowls and plates and stacked them up on a tray before she disappeared slowly into the kitchen. Her coming and going instantly sobered up the mood at the table.

Kelvin was the first to say something. "It's true, isn't?" he said, looking at mom and dad. "If the two of you had stayed in Hong Kong, you could easily have been that woman."

It was an odd thing to say. My mom was visibly offended by it. Even though my parents are not wealthy *per se*, they live comfortably in Toronto. Social security payments from the Canadian government cover their daily expenses. Healthcare is free of charge. Every day my dad drives his car around town and meets his friends for coffee. My mom tends to her garden and does *tai chi* in the city park across from the house. They lead a charmed retirement life.

At the same time, I understood where Kelvin was coming from. I have lived in enough places around the world to know that Hong Kong is no city for old people. I have seen more senior citizens picking through the trash here than anywhere else. If my parents had spent their retirement in Hong Kong, their story would have had a very different ending. They would have had a lot more to complain about than uneven sidewalks and the stifling heat.

So I jumped to my brother's defense. "What Kelvin is trying to say," I paraphrased as I refilled everyone's teacup, "is that old people in Hong Kong are vulnerable because there isn't a safety net for them to fall back on. He doesn't mean *you* necessarily, but people your age in general."

With that, I tried to segue into the hypothetical. I wanted to make an intellectual exercise out of an uncomfortable conversation.

"Now that we're on the subject, let's talk about growing old in Hong Kong," I said, as if addressing my students. "Imagine you two were living here but you couldn't depend on any of us because, say, we'd all moved overseas. What would you do?"

"I don't know, but you all had better look for cover when lightning strikes!" my mom warned, invoking an old Chinese belief that filially impious children should brace for a reckoning from God.

"Come on, mom, this is a *hypothetical*! Just go along with it."

My dad started to show some interest. "Housing is the biggest problem," he spoke from experience. "In your scenario, where would we live?"

"For argument's sake, let's say you still had your old apartment in Tin Hau," I answered, "but you didn't have much else because you'd used all your savings to pay off the mortgage."

I needed to simplify the exercise. If my parents didn't have their own place, they would have to get in line for public housing. Although the wait time for an elderly couple is shorter than for others, it would still have taken them at least five years to be assigned a government flat. During those five long years, the only solution would have been a subdivided unit the size of a prison cell. We call them "coffin homes" and for good reason.

"Since all our children have abandoned us," my mom grumbled, still having trouble divorcing her emotions from the exercise, "we'd apply for welfare."

Without any assets or income, my parents would both be eligible for social security. Their self-use home would be excluded from the asset test as long as they promised not to sell it while receiving welfare checks.

"Together your mom and I would get around HK$6,000 (US$770) a month from the government," my dad surmised. It was an educated guess based on what he heard from friends who had applied.

"Let's work with that number then," I said, pleased that our discussion was finally going somewhere. "Utilities would cost you HK$1,000 (US$130) a month. Cell phones and cable TV would be another HK$1,000."

"We could share one cell phone – for emergency," my dad said sensibly. "Also, we could watch free television and forget about cable. Beggars can't be choosers, you know."

"And no AC either," my mom chimed in. I was impressed by the sacrifice, knowing her intolerance for hot weather. "That alone would save hundreds every month. A golden bull should cover all the monthly outlays." "Golden bull" is the Cantonese nickname for a $1,000 bill.

My mom took a sip of tea and continued. "Oh, I almost forgot about property tax. That'd be HK$300 (US$38) a month. It's a tenement building, so there wouldn't be any management fee. We'd still need to fork out about HK$200 (US$25) to have the trash picked up." Those penny pinching days in Hong Kong were all coming back to her now.

Kelvin noticed that mom was no longer upset with him and he joined in: "Alright, that'd leave HK$4,500 (US$580) for everything else."

I did some simple arithmetic in my head and summarized, "Each of you would have HK$75 (US$10) a day to spend on food and public transport." Suddenly I felt guilty for taking taxis everywhere without another thought. A single cab ride would have burned up their entire daily allowance.

"Old folks like us get special rates on buses. It only costs HK$2 (US$0.25) per ride!" my dad cheered. "We'd figure out a way to make do with HK$75. We're tough cookies."

That I knew. My parents escaped the Civil War in China and struggled through the 1950s and 60s in nascent Hong Kong. They raised five children on a meager income and managed to send all of them to college. Calling them tough would be an understatement.

"I agree with your father – I'd go to the wet markets just before the vendors close for the night," my mom shared her time honored money saving tips. "That's how the poor put food on the table in Hong Kong."

She was right. Street vendors slash prices every night and sell leftover produce by the pile. A basketful of slightly bruised pears sell for HK$10 (US$1.30). Two dead fish for HK$15 (US$2). Until recently, senior citizens would wait outside supermarket chains like Wellcome and Park'n Shop and scour the trash for discarded but still edible food expiring that day. To discourage free loaders, however, supermarket staff now deliberately destroy unsold food. They are known to douse chlorine on bread and shred vegetables into unsalvageable bits. Unbeknownst to most citizens, a crime against nature is committed every night across the city. Cutthroat business owners are well advised to heed my mom's advice and look for cover when lightning strikes.

"Wait a minute," my dad suddenly remembered something important and turned to my mom, "what about your blood pressure and cholesterol? Even with free healthcare at government clinics, your medication would still cost money!"

End-of-day bargains at the wet markets

"Not to mention all the unexpected expenses," Kelvin pursued. "What if the refrigerator broke and needed to be replaced? What if there was a leak in the bathroom, the neighbor downstairs complained and a plumber had to be sent?"

"We really would need a job," my dad sighed. "but no one would hire an old man with a bad leg."

My father's grim employment prospects have less to do with his disability than the obsolescence of his skills. He was a newspaper illustrator before he retired some 20 years ago, but 9 out of 10 of his employers have gone out of business. The industry has changed beyond recognition since he left Hong Kong. So has the rest of the labor market.

"*I* can work!" my mom pounded her chest. "I don't have many skills but I can at least get a job at a restaur..."

She stopped herself mid-sentence and looked at Kelvin. She started to blush despite herself. It dawned her that her son wasn't being disrespectful when he compared her to the dish lady. He was being realistic.

My parents always feel grateful for their lives in Toronto, but that night at the Chinese restaurant, they were more grateful than usual. We all had Kelvin to thank for that.

住在玻璃屋的人

Those Who Live in Glass Houses

In a city where space is at a premium, where a luxury apartment on the Peak costs more than the GDP of a small nation, and where a serviced apartment in Wanchai can rent for three times the average household income, there is a surprisingly easy way to create space. With a few buckets of cement and a bamboo scaffolding, a contractor can turn your balcony into an extra bedroom or add a solarium on the other side of the back wall. If you live on the top floor, you can even build an entire glass house on the rooftop complete with its own kitchen and bathroom. When it comes to creating livable space, your imagination – and audacity – are the only limit.

An extra bedroom in the making

Unauthorized building alterations are everywhere in Hong Kong. They are also against the law. Like jaywalking and downloading movies online, the building of illegal structures is one of those offences that many commit but no one expects to get caught. While a majority of the city's illegal structures are safe, many of them pose fire and other public safety risks. Every now and then we hear news stories about fallen balconies and collapsed canopies that succumbed to a rainstorm. Those who lost their lives to illegal structures achieve martyrdom in our collective struggle against the property cartel, for they are the very reason why illegal structures exist in the first place.

The problem of unauthorized building works is particularly egregious in the rural areas of the New Territories. In 1972, the colonial government introduced the so-called "small house" (丁屋) policy to get buy-in from New Territories villagers for its urban development plans. The scheme grants every male descendant of indigenous lineage the right to build a standalone house on government land when he turns 18. As the name of the policy would suggest, these houses are meant to be small, capped at three stories and 700 square feet per floor. In addition to being overtly sexist, however, the controversial policy created a massive headache for subsequent administrations, as land supply fails to keep up with the male birth rate. Motivated by greed or necessity, many right-holders take the policy as a *carte blanche* to build whatever their hearts desire, putting up four or five-story houses, each with an obligatory glass house sitting on the rooftop for self-use or for rent. When a recent report by the Ombudsman Office prompted the government to finally take action against construction violations, villagers responded with mob anger and threatened to wage a "bloody revolution" the likes of which the city had never seen.

The villager's bellicose rhetoric might have been over the top, but their sentiment is understandable – for who among us is without sin?

Like millions others in Hong Kong, my family and I were once beneficiaries of illegal structures. Back in the 1960s, my parents lived in a rental apartment on the rooftop of a tenement building in Wanchai. Built with plywood and corrugated metal, the unit cost HK$100 (US$13) a month, roughly 10% of my father's income at the time. Though the tenement building was torn down and rebuilt many years ago, my parents still speak fondly of their "penthouse" apartment where the living room and outdoor garden were separated by a swinging screen door.

During the early 1970s my family moved into a brick and mortar apartment in Tin Hau, finally a legal abode we could call our own. Even so, there were two basic house rules to which we were forced to abide: no jumping in the kitchen and no more than one person in it at any given time. Mounted on the exterior wall and supported by cantilever beams, the kitchen was a metal cage packed with heavy appliances and overhead cabinetry. Add a microwave oven and the whole thing might tumble like a free fall ride at Ocean Park. Fortunately for us, nothing of the sort ever happened, not to our kitchen or to any of our neighbors' similarly built structures above and below us.

Our longstanding culture of illegal structures has come under intense media scrutiny in recent years. Just when the small house saga was pushing the city to the brink of a civil war, the press discovered a spate of building violations by high profile politicians. The issue is widely believed to have tipped the balance in the 2012 chief executive election. Henry Tang, Beijing's favored candidate, was caught hiding an illegal basement underneath his Kowloon Tong residence. His opponent C.Y. Leung used the scandal to attack his credibility and it eventually cost Tang the election. Ironically, as soon as Leung took office, the new chief himself was forced to take down an illegal storeroom and glass enclosure at his Peak mansion. It is said that those who live in glass houses should not throw stones; those who literally live in glass houses, like Leung and many other government officials before him, lack the moral authority to make us follow rules that they themselves have broken.

Illegal structures are a way of life in Hong Kong. The recent turn of events has forced the government to confront a social issue that has long been swept under the rug. Neither a one-time amnesty to exempt all existing unauthorized structures from demolition nor a pay-per-structure scheme would work. The former would lead to a mad rush to get new structures in before the door is permanently closed, while the latter raises fairness issues between those who can pay their way around the law and those who can't. Most importantly, neither approach addresses the fundamental issue of public safety. It appears that the government has little choice but to stay its course and use its limited resources to crack down on structures that pose an immediate danger. Short of solving the fundamental housing problem in Hong Kong, whatever the government decides to do will only treat the symptoms and not the cause.

All the Rage

I was standing in line at Citibank to deposit a check. It was lunch time in Central and the branch was bursting at the seams. The customer in front of me, a middle-aged gentleman in a tailored suit, asked to take out five thousand Euros in cash. Behind the counter was a teller who couldn't have been more than six months out of university. Her name was proudly embossed on her lapel pin: Trainee.

"I'm sorry, Mr. Cheung," said Trainee to the gentleman, before explaining that she didn't have enough Euros and that a day's notice was normally required for withdrawals over a certain amount. Bank policy. She asked him to either collect the cash the next day or try the main branch.

What followed, however, was an unstoppable tirade from the not-so-gentle-man over a situation he called an "outrage" and a "waste of everyone's time," all delivered with the usual hysterics: clenched jaw, flapping arms and a face as red as a ripe tomato.

This Bruce Banner had transformed into his monstrous alter ego.

"Where is your manager?" the Hulk rumbled. By now, everyone at the branch was staring at the man with one thought on their minds: there is a rageaholic in the house.

We are too willing to unleash our inner Hulk

The Christian faith regards anger as one of the seven deadly sins. Buddhists call it one of the "three poisons" that causes human suffering. Abominable as it is, rage is an evolutionary instinct, a biologically programmed "fight or flight" response to external threats. It is also a necessary step in the way we cope with bad news. According to the celebrated Kübler-Ross model, grievers go through a series of emotional stages: denial, anger, bargaining, depression, and acceptance. Nevertheless, many of us prefer to wallow in the second stage and have no qualms doing it in public places like a crowded bank in the middle of Central. With blood rushing to our heads and our hearts pounding like *taiko* drums, the only stages we know are yelling, cursing, name calling and threatening. Bargaining will have to wait.

Mobile phones and social networks have shrunk our personal space. Being constantly in each other's face has shortened our fuse, thinned our patience and made urban rage an epidemic. Psychologists estimate that people lose their cool on average of 10 to 14 times a day. What used to be a genetically-coded survival mechanism is now triggered almost hourly by minor annoyances like getting cut off in traffic or missing an elevator. When it comes to road rage, air rage and office rage, we are both victims and offenders. It feels as though everyone around us is in a constant state of smoldering anger.

Going berserk comes with a price. Whereas laughter releases endorphins, which elevate our mood, anger leads to a surge in adrenaline and cortisol, which do just the opposite. Rage-related ailments include headaches, indigestion, high blood pressure, heart attack and stroke. A wise man once said that everyone starts with a life span of 125 years, but every minor tantrum he throws takes one day off, and every major blow-out takes two.

If getting mad is bad for us, then why do we still do it?

The simple answer is pride. Anger conveys two clear social messages: we are under threat and we won't take it lying down. When a taxi driver takes us for a ride and says he did it to avoid traffic, we feel obligated to assert our manhood by going postal on him. Our pride is most at risk when the threat is prejudice based, such as when a coworker cracks a joke about our waistlines or a sexist property broker only talks to the husband.

Sometimes the prejudice is imagined. Mr. Cheung's manic episode at Citibank was perhaps stoked by a nagging suspicion that the teller's response had less to do with bank policy and more to do with his own social station. He wondered if Li Ka-shing would be told to "come back tomorrow." Then came the existential self-doubt: Why am I stuck in my dead end job? What am I doing here exchanging money for my French boss? Psychiatrists say that when you blow up, you are only trying to relieve the contempt you feel for yourself. Right, Mr. Cheung?

While some rageaholics explode to preserve their pride, others do so for purely utilitarian reasons. They do what a three-year-old child would do: stomp his feet to get what he wants. It works because anger often legitimizes behavior. Researchers have found that people in negotiations tend to concede more to the angry side than to the placid side. They have also found that people with angry facial expressions are perceived to be more powerful and of higher social status. These findings explain why so much of our aggression is directed at our coworkers and people in the service industry. Whether it is in the office or at a restaurant, it is the squeaky wheel that gets the oil and the angry bird that gets the worm.

Like it or not, we live in a society where a little door slamming or desk pounding can go a long way. This phenomenon is particularly prevalent in Asia, where people tend to avoid confrontation and, as a result, the cost of public rage is low. After all, what can a defenseless Thai waitress do when you lash out at her for not giving you a window-side table?

Over time, Asian pacifism has spawned a new species called the "ugly expat." They are the subset of foreigners living in Asia who exploit this cultural arbitrage. They think of themselves as rock stars and that none of the social rules apply to them. They make a scene, get their way and brag about it to their friends. But pit bulls beware: pull that kind of horse manure back home in New York, London or Sydney and they will make you pay. Just ask Alec Baldwin, who famously got booted off a plane for acting aggressively toward a flight attendant, or Russell Crowe, who was arrested and charged with second degree assault for throwing a telephone at a hotel employee.

I admit I don't have the best of tempers. Put me in front of a rude waitress or a foul mouthed bus driver, and I won't hesitate to roll up my proverbial sleeves and start a screaming match. While I justify my feistiness by calling it a one man crusade to "teach these people a lesson" for the betterment of mankind, in truth it probably has more to do with defending my pride or wanting to be a squeaky wheel. And while as a lawyer I am accustomed to being adversarial, I am aware of the effect an unpleasant confrontation can have on my dinner guests or travel companions.

Worse still, rageaholics often have trouble switching off their anger, even when dealing with friends and family. I am known to let the heat of the moment get the best of me and can be too willing to damage a relationship just to make a point. The wounds may heal over time, but the scars remain. It took me years of practice to lock up my green monster and unleash it only to protect my loved ones. The warning label on the fire escape hammer sums it up well: use only in an actual emergency.

Nowadays whenever I am about to throw a fit, I make myself count to 30 or name all the American presidents since Teddy Roosevelt. By the time I get to Harry Truman, I will have forgotten what has gotten me so worked up in the first place. It sounds simple but it works every time.

As for the hothead at Citibank, he finally got what he wanted. The branch manager showed up moments later to do damage control. He called the main branch to have the Euros delivered to Mr. Cheung within 20 minutes. So the angry man triumphed once again. Or so he thought, as did King Pyrrhus after he defeated the Romans only to discover that his victory came at an unanticipated and devastating cost. Take it from a recovering rageaholic.

Calling it Quits

I

It's 9:30 on a Monday night. You are waiting for the bus to take you home after another long, dreary day in the office. Your head droops to the side, your shoulders slump, and your leather briefcase sags with the weight of existential angst. The woman in front of you pulls a soggy pastry out of a wrinkled Starbucks bag and takes a bite. You think to yourself: I can make a better one and sell it for half the price. The dream of running your own bakery and wallowing in patisserie bliss once again rushes to your head. No more 13-hour days, no more suits and ties, no more crowded buses and microwave dinners. Leather briefcase be damned!

What you just read is a familiar scene to many salaried men and women. Tired of the ball and chain of a desk job, you fantasize about a "Plan B" to take you out of the rat race and put your God given talent to use. If baking is not your thing, then it may be designing jewelry, becoming a wedding photographer or running an event planning service from home. How about opening a bicycle repair shop or a bed and breakfast on a far flung island? The daily grind of a dead end job, exacerbated by that old adage "you only live once" (or "YOLO" in short), is enough for you to seriously consider walking into the boss's office and giving him the boot. Entrepreneurship be praised!

He wants out

Self-employment is not always by choice. With a sputtering world economy and China now showing signs of a slowdown, job security is at a low ebb. Just ask the Japanese. When the axe falls and you find yourself downsized or made redundant, you tell yourself that all is not lost. It is a sign from God. You remember the stories of Oprah Winfrey, Steve Jobs and other billionaires who got fired before making it big. You also remember the way friends and family rave about your cupcakes and tell you how gifted you are. So instead of updating your résumé, you empty your bank account and sign a two-year lease for a retail space. As the smell of freshly baked croissants fills the store, you give yourself the familiar pep talk: Losing my job is the best thing that ever happened to me!

About a year ago, my cousin Alfred quit his job as a marketing executive and opened his own beauty clinic offering facial and lipo treatments. Leaning on his industry experience and an MBA, Alfred worked out a detailed business plan, sourced doctors and technicians and took out a bank loan to purchase state of the art equipment. Business was going well as far as a startup goes. Sales climbed steadily in the first quarter and he even broke even in the fourth month. Then the numbers started to go south and Alfred began to panic. The clinic was hemorrhaging cash due to rent, wages and utilities bills. The mounting financial pressure took a personal toll. He developed a stomach ulcer and had to take sleeping pills before going to bed. He became impatient and irritable. After another six months, Alfred wanted out. He figured that no personal dream is big enough to give up his health and family. He closed down the clinic and began looking for a new job.

My cousin's eleven-month odyssey in the entrepreneurial world is not uncommon. Plan B can be a Herculean feat. Statistics show that one out of two businesses fails within twelve months and eight out of ten fail within three years. In many cases, failure is caused not by bad products or weak sales, but by the lack of an adequate capital cushion. The fact that most seed money comes from personal savings and bank borrowings can make the first time entrepreneur particularly risk averse. He would rather cut his losses than throw good money after bad.

Other than financial risks, self-employment is fraught with hidden peril. What happens if a customer gets food poisoning after eating your cupcakes or sues you for botched wedding pictures? In Alfred's case, because he couldn't afford expensive liability insurance, he was one medical mishap away from a multi-million dollar negligence suit. Earlier this year, several people in Hong Kong were arrested for copyright infringement, after being caught reselling counterfeit handbags they purchased from Taobao, China's online marketplace. When it comes to running your own business, ignorance is no defense.

Then there are the personal and emotional costs. My cousin thought that by being his own boss, he would have more personal time for his family. Boy, was he mistaken! While Alfred's title might have been Managing Director, he was also his own decorator, secretary, janitor and IT guy. He spent many a night alone in the clinic vacuuming the carpet and setting up computer terminals. He was pulling 18-hour work days and was too stressed to even have a normal dinner with his children. Family vacations were out of the question.

That's not all. Turning your part time interest into a full time job can be the quickest way to kill a passion. Many freelance musicians and photographers who have "gone pro" discover that mixing play and work is no fun. To put food on the table, even the high and mighty have to get down and dirty. Unless your name is Bob Dylan or Annie Leibovitz, you're probably not above writing commercial jingles or taking pictures for supermarket flyers. As if that's not humbling enough, there is the risk of discovering that you aren't as gifted as you thought you were. Praise from friends and family can be out of courtesy. The real world, on the other hand, is a far less forgiving place. The realization that you aren't cut out to do what you love – be that baking or writing music – can be a crushing blow to the ego.

Several weeks after he ended his business, Alfred got a job offer from a Fortune 100 pharmaceutical company. Thanks to a supportive wife and a strong résumé, he was able to land on his two feet. My cousin joined an increasing number of entrepreneurs who choose to return to a desk job, a move that is dubbed "Plan C." And why not? Plan C offers a long list of benefits that cubical captives often overlook: a steady paycheck, paid vacation days, health plans and a support staff to take care of your mundane paperwork. Surely there are difficult bosses and unreasonable clients in every organization, but that's the devil you know, and at least the devil doesn't bother you once you go home to your family.

I have a passion for many things and writing is one of them. Each time I see the half-finished manuscript of my next book sitting on my desk, the thought of quitting my job and becoming a full time writer crosses my mind. Before my thoughts drift too far, however, the realist in me reels me in. An inner voice will tell me that Plan B is a lot like exercising: I only need to do it a few times a week to feel good about myself. Somewhere between Plan A and Plan B, there is an attainable balance.

"Don't make rash decisions," Alfred said to me at a recent family dinner, "Start something on the side to test the waters while you still have a paying job." Sound advice. I call that Plan A-and-a-Half.

II

My older siblings are professionals in their 40s and early 50s. They have hunkered down at the same companies for decades and seen their stress levels rise in lockstep with their seniority. With their children heading off to college, they have one thought on their minds constantly: retirement. The earlier the better. It is a topic of conversation that dominates every family dinner and gets all of us scribbling numbers on the back of a napkin. On that napkin is a game plan, an exit strategy and a light at the end of the tunnel. It is our midlife euphoria.

The idea of being emancipated from our cubicle and lying on a sandy beach all day is enough to make any overworked middle-aged parent crack a smile. On the other hand, the notion that we must work another 15 to 20 years before reaping what we sow seems unpalatable, if not downright depressing. We want to taste the fruits of life while we still can, when our knees are strong enough to ski and our bodies are not too droopy for swimwear. Among Gen Xers like me and my siblings, there is a growing backlash against "affluenza," the social disease that keeps us on an endless pursuit of wealth and material possessions. Many are coming to the realization that a simple, happy life beats going in circles chasing a bigger home and a flashier sports car. Being a quitter has never been so cool. Doing it at 45 is even cooler.

Early retirement is a numbers game. As any financial planner would advise, there are three questions we need to ask ourselves:

1. How long do we expect to live?
2. How much money do we need each month?
3. What inflation rate should we factor into our calculation?

Question 1 is straightforward. Government statistics put the male life expectancy at 80. It is as good an estimate as any fortuneteller can give us. That means if we retire at 45, we'll have to finance a retirement that lasts almost as many years as we have lived. What happens if all those spin classes and multivitamin supplements pay off and we live beyond the age of 80? Do not fret. If we run out of money in our twilight years, by all means sell the apartment we live in. Contrary to Asian belief, we are not obligated to pass real estate to our children.

The question of monthly income requires a bit more thought. The best clues lie in our pre-retirement spending patterns – the aggregate amount we currently spend on food, clothing, entertainment and travel each month. While the number may vary significantly depending on our lifestyle, it tends to hover somewhere around HK$25,000 (US$3,200) based on my own finances and discussions with family and like-minded friends. The amount excludes the monthly mortgage payment (we strongly advise against retirement before your home is paid off) and assumes there are no expensive hobbies. If yachting or art collecting is your thing, then early retirement is probably not right for you.

Don't even think about it

Inflation is a tricky business. It ebbs and flows with the economic cycle and is highly dependent on our spending habits. Drinkers, drivers and timepiece lovers face much higher inflation as the prices of alcohol, gasoline and luxury watches tend to rise faster than those of other goods. It also differs by country. The average inflation rate in Hong Kong since 1980 is around 5% per annum, whereas the U.S. Federal Reserve has a target inflation rate of

2%. Japan, on the other hand, has been experiencing deflation since the 1990s. As a general matter, a moderate rate of 3% is a good rule of thumb.

Plugging these numbers into a simple annuity formula gives us the ballpark figure of HK$18 million (US$2.3 million). This is our bronze parachute, the piggybank we need in order to retire at 45 with a monthly income of HK$25,000 (US$3,200) in real terms. It is the magic number we should scribble on a yellow sticky and pin on our computer screen as an incentive to work harder and save more. The number may look daunting to some and altogether unreachable to others. If that's the case, reduce the monthly income amount or raise the retirement age until the target becomes achievable. For instance, the lump sum figure will drop to HK$14 million (US$1.8 million) if retirement is postponed to the age of 50.

That's all the number crunching we need for now. Before we start drawing up that bucket list, a couple of reality checks are in order.

First, we need to be disciplined, both before and after retirement. While we still have a job, we need to come up with a saving plan and stick to it. That means no more impulse buys at the end-of-season sale or splurging on luxury hotels on the Christmas trip, no matter how financially invincible we feel while we are still on the payroll.

Once we leave our job, we must be prepared to cut back on conveniences like taking a taxi instead of mass transit. Flying coach shouldn't feel like an imposition any more. It is called "downshifting," the reduction in unnecessary spending as a way to focus on quality of life instead of quantity. Each dollar not spent should go to a slush fund to cover unexpected outlays that sneak up on the retiree when he can least afford them. Just a few days ago, I received a notice from my building's management committee demanding HK$50,000 (US$6,400) from each owner to install new elevators, payable in 30 days. It's not the kind of news a retiree wants to hear when he is already pinching his pennies. And while we are still healthy, we should take out an insurance policy that covers critical illnesses. It's no fun having to choose between medical care and food.

Second, the joy of early retirement may be overrated. The *schadenfreude* pleasure of knowing that our friends are toiling in the office while we read the morning newspaper in our pajamas will wear off after a few months. When every day is like Sunday, it doesn't take long before we start feeling out of touch with the real world. The loss of a daily routine, coupled with the need to downshift from a lifestyle we have grown accustomed to, can throw us emotionally off balance. Also, researchers have found that retired people lose their memories and cognitive skills over time, no matter how many crossword puzzles and Sudoku they do each day to keep their minds sharp. To give us a sense of purpose and stay mentally active, we need to set measurable goals for our post-retirement years. This may sound a bit strange, but deadlines and a moderate dose of stress can go a long way to keep us sane. Let's face it, we city folks are gluttons for punishment.

Early retirement sounds like fun, but we need to do it for the right reason and in the right way. It is not something we should rush into because we had a bad day at work. Like many other things in life, it is a double-edged sword. While it relieves us from the stress of a full time job, it replaces it with stress of another kind – the constant fear that we are running out of money because of poor planning or unforeseen circumstances. If my siblings and I are any indication, after all these years of talking and scribbling, none of us has summoned enough courage to take the plunge.

數
綿
羊

Counting Sheep

It is said that the best things in life are free. Children's smiles, glorious sunsets and the soothing sounds of ocean waves. Of all the simple pleasures in life, sleeping is the most beneficial to our bodies and minds. It is also the most underrated. When alpha cities like Hong Kong, Tokyo and New York fall over each other vying for the dubious title of The City that Doesn't Sleep, it is the citizens who pay the price. Our mounting workload, over-developed social life and that black hole called the Internet all contribute to our sleep deficit. Every now and then when we get to stay in bed for a couple of extra hours on a lazy Sunday morning, we are reminded what a real treat those forty winks are.

An average person in Hong Kong sleeps 6.6 hours a day. That means for every one of us who gets the recommended eight hours of z's, there is a poor soul scraping by with just five. While some blame it on the Asian work culture, others point to runaway property prices that are sending ever more urban exiles to remote neighborhoods, which lengthens their daily commute and shortens their sleep time.

Businesses feel the sting of our skewed property market just as much. Since McDonald's went 24 hours in Hong Kong several years ago, many noodle houses and *cha chaan teng* (茶餐廳) – our quirky local cafés – have jumped into the fray of retail insomnia. Across the city, shops are staying open later and later into the night to make up for rent increases. After the store clerk finally locks up for the night, there is still an hour long bus ride and 30 minutes of late night television before he hits the sack.

Whereas a lot of attention has been paid to diet and exercise, few take bedtime seriously. Sleep is the first thing that gets cut whenever we need to make up for time. According to *The Inner Canon of the Emperor* (《黃帝內經》), the sacred Chinese medical treatise written two millennia ago, the body begins its self-healing at around 11pm at night, when the *qi* (氣) in the liver regenerates itself.

The Inner Canon of the Emperor *goes back to the Han Dynasty*

The restorative function of sleep is also well documented in Western medicine. Our body follows the circadian clock, the timekeeper within us that controls our wakefulness and the schedule of bodily functions. Studies have shown that the kidneys do most of their recharging and recovering between 11pm and 1am, and that the gallbladder removes toxins during this period. Studies have also shown that sleep plays an integral role in wound healing and memory processing. On the other hand, sleep deprivation disrupts the circadian rhythm and can cause headaches, irritability and memory lapses, while a chronic lack of sleep can lead to obesity, diabetes and heart disease.

Sleep is as much a science as it is an art. To appreciate the art, we need to treat it with respect and care. I consider myself a sleep enthusiast and I practice strict "sleep hygiene." For starters, my bed is always impeccably made and the surrounding area free of clutter and strewn clothes. I have opaque window covering to block out all external light, and I still wear an eye mask for good measure. I keep the television, laptop, iPad and other electronic devices out of the bedroom. When in doubt, I follow the simple advice from the UK Sleep Council: the bed should be for rest and sex and nothing else. Amen to that.

A physician once told me that if a person falls asleep within 10 minutes of going to bed or snoozes more than twice in the morning, then he is sleep deprived. The second part of that statement alarms me because I am a pathological snoozer and an unusually sound sleeper. In college, I was known to slumber through fire alarms. I gave my dorm-mates permission to douse water on my face to wake me up for class. Thanks to my trigger happy fingers with the snooze button, I managed to miss nearly all my 9am classes and one of my final exams in my freshman year. Old habits die hard, and even now, showing up at work on time remains a daily challenge. The price I pay for those extra 15 minutes of snoozing is a 20-yard "walk of shame" from the main door to my office at the end of the hall.

Because I value my shuteye, I have deep sympathy for people who have trouble sleeping. Insomnia is a curse I would not wish on even my worst enemies. I have friends who, despite therapy and medication, remain insomniac for years. They tell me heartbreaking stories about how their condition holds them back in their career and denies them the simple pleasures in life. Every once in a while, I get a taste of what these people go through. Whenever I make the regrettable mistake of drinking a caffeinated beverage after 8pm, it is *Sleepless in Hong Kong* all over again. I will spend hours willing myself to sleep. As every insomniac can attest: the harder one tries, the more awake one becomes. When dawn breaks and the early birds start to chirp, I know all is lost. It's a miserable experience.

Randy Gardner from San Diego, California holds the official world record for the longest period anyone has gone without sleep: 11 straight days. Gardner's record is believed to have been broken by a Vietnamese farmer, Thai Ngoc, who claims that a bout of fever has left him awake for over three decades. Although it appears that Ngoc would be 33% more productive than the rest of us, he is not one to be envied. Researchers have found that while income level has almost no correlation with happiness, sleep does. Sleep and happiness form a positive feedback loop: more of one leads to more of the other. As I burn the midnight oil trying to finish this essay on a Sunday night, with another grueling work week about to start in mere hours, I am more convinced than ever that sleep, the natural state of unconsciousness we go through every day, holds the key to our quality of life.

May we all sleep well and prosper.

Down but Not Out

My big sister Ada is one of the bubbliest people I know. She has a contagious laugh and takes a genuine interest in people. A consummate hostess, she loves entertaining and throws elaborate dinner parties, the kind that are lifted straight out of a Martha Stewart magazine. On paper, the forty-something mother of two has it all: a loving family, a well paying job and a comfortable life. It is therefore all the more shocking when she told me recently that she is suffering from depression.

It all began shortly after she got a promotion at work. At first it was the usual urban angst: headaches, low energy and erratic eating habits – signs that she had reached a higher rung on the corporate ladder. Then her mood swings began. At home, she would sit idly in a corner and cry without provocation. Things she used to enjoy, like shopping, cooking and traveling, lost their allure. She resented pseudo-spiritual advice from friends to "count your blessings" and "stay positive," as if the human mind had some kind of on/off switch with smiley faces all over it. At work, any disagreement became a personal affront. Even a simple "Are you all right?" from a concerned coworker would seem like a criticism, enough to send her into an inconsolable sob. Her harshest critic, however, was herself. Each depressive episode would leave her feeling more incompetent and more worthless, plunging her deeper into the downward spiral.

Determined to be a good mother, a good wife and a good employee, Ada kept her condition to herself. Over time, she developed a system to conceal her emotions. She minimized human interactions and learned to flash a smile on reflex. The ladies' room at the office was the only sanctuary where she could take a break from her daily act. It was all working fairly well until her breakdowns began happening with such debilitating frequency that impeded even normal functioning. She realized she could no longer fight the battle alone. She decided to seek professional help.

My sister's ordeal is an increasingly common phenomenon in a megalopolis like Hong Kong. Depression is often caused by stress – there is plenty of that to go around here – but triggered by something bigger, such as physical or emotional trauma. In Ada's case, as she would later find out from her physician, her malaise was the result of a hormonal imbalance, exacerbated by increased demands at work and at home, where both of her children were growing rapidly into adolescence. Other common triggers include pregnancy, divorce and a death in the family. Several years ago, one of my best friends L was diagnosed with manic depression after his father passed away in the same month he broke up with his girlfriend of seven years. Similar to what Ada experienced, it was the stress from a job change that finally pushed L over the mental cliff. On several occasions, he attempted suicide by climbing onto the ledge outside his apartment window.

Hong Kong is a perfect petri dish for mental disorder. The island is overcrowded and overworked. It is where self-worth is measured by professional success and professional success can only be achieved within our cubicle prisons. It is where social comparison conspires with urban claustrophobia to create a seething cauldron of stress. According to a recent survey, one in three people in the city suffers from some form of mental illness. Since stress is so much a part of life here, citizens are conditioned to suck it up and grind it out. That's the way most of us cope with personal problems in this part of the world. We would see a fortuneteller before looking for a therapist.

The city can do that to you

Once depression sets in, few are able to recognize the symptoms and fewer still bother or dare to get help. Despite growing social awareness of mental health in Hong Kong – largely as a result of several local celebrities coming out of the closet and openly discussing their struggles – the topic remains taboo. Depression is still a dirty word. It is either an excuse for the lazy or a condition of the crazy. Admitting to having depression in the workplace, or simply asking for time off to treat it, can be a career limiting move and a social death sentence. It is in the context of this don't ask don't tell culture that Ada decided to talk to me about her experience. "Enough people have suffered in silence and the closet is running out of space," she said during our interview.

So what are the signs of depression? Google the words "depression" and "symptoms" and you will get more or less the same laundry list: fatigue, insomnia, mood swings, appetite loss, low self-esteem and guilt. Unfortunately for the unaware, the list is vague and unhelpful. Much of it coincides with symptoms of the seasonal flu. And unfortunately for us Asians, almost all of the medical literature is based on Western cases. The only sure way of knowing is to talk to a doctor, and you should do so if the symptoms last more than two to three weeks. "There is no shame in getting help," Ada urged, "but only in letting your ego and fears stand between you and a normal life."

To complicate things, not all depression is created equal. It varies in its symptoms, severity and treatment. Ada was diagnosed with clinical depression, also known as unipolar disorder. Antidepressants like Prozac or Zoloft are often prescribed but they can be substituted with talk therapy. What my friend L has, on the other hand, is the much more serious manic depression, or bipolar disorder, a condition characterized by alternating periods of depression and mania. If left untreated, it can lead to delusions, psychosis and even suicide. L has been on a strict regimen of mood stabilizing drugs since his diagnosis and will likely stay on it for life.

To those suffering from clinical depression, which is by far the most common type of mental disorder, Ada offered advice based on her firsthand experience. "Talk to someone you trust," she stressed. And talk she did. She started by telling her sister and confidant Margaret, who lent a much needed ear and suggested medical help. Next, she talked to her family doctor and was promptly referred to a specialist. Ada found it helpful to bring her husband to some of the therapy sessions. After all, two heads are better than one, especially when fighting an illness that requires heaps of understanding and patience from the other half.

At the risk of hurting her career, my sister decided to share her struggles with her boss, the one who gave her the job promotion that started it all. He not only gave Ada ample time off to rest, but much to her surprise, he reciprocated by sharing his own experience with depression. It turned out that the ailment is much more common than Ada had thought.

A year after my sister began therapy, she is back to her old vivacious self, thanks to her support system – her family, doctor, colleagues and friends – and her own courage to acknowledge and confront her illness. She admits she is not completely out of the woods. "Something like this stays with you forever," she confessed, "but at least I know how to deal with it if it relapses." For now, depressive episodes are few and far between. Each time they occur, she makes an entry in her journal to discuss with her therapist. She also exercises regularly, for "a healthy mind starts with a healthy body." She chuckled at her own cliché, that same contagious laugh that I love and miss. I ended our interview with a hug, and told her what an incredibly brave and honorable thing she did to have her story told.

Part 2
Our Culture

The Storm Cometh

Hong Kong is relatively free from natural disasters. We don't have earthquakes, blizzards or volcanic eruptions. We are spared the kind of sweeping destruction and massive death toll that plague many of our neighbors. What we do have are the half-dozen tropical storms that come our way during the summer months. The more powerful ones are called typhoons, with wind gusts reaching 120 kilometers per hour.

On average, we get six to seven tropical storms every year from May through September. The weather systems originate in the Pacific and travel westward before making landfall along the South China coast. Our city is only one of the many stops they make on their ocean traversing path. By the time the storms pass through our city, frequently they will have already wreaked havoc in the Philippines or Taiwan.

Typhoons are a way of life in Hong Kong and we have developed a tried and tested early warning system to minimize casualties and property damage. There are four typhoon signals based on wind speed and proximity, from the lowest T1 and T3 to T8 and the highest T10. While newcomers to the city often mistake our storm signals for the *Terminator* movie franchise, locals find the system equally confounding. For instance, we don't know why there is no T2 or T5. We suspect the scale might have been designed by the same genius who invented the tennis scoring system. Also, storm signals are never just issued; they are "hoisted." It came from the old practice of hanging drums and balloons at different locations along the harbor to warn fishermen. The word is incongruous in today's world of smartphones and tablet computers. It evokes images of halberds and crossbows in a medieval battle.

What's more, it seems arbitrary that only T8 and T10 behoove a citywide shutdown and give citizens a day off. The double standard makes T1 and T3 feel like the ugly sisters that no one loves. In 1992, after torrential rains paralyzed the city, the colonial government introduced a similar warning system for rainstorms. Rain signals are color-coded according to the amount of precipitation per hour – amber, red and black – but only black rains result in work and school stoppages. So amber and red join T1 and T3 in an ugly sisterhood that elicits a collective "boohoo" from the city.

In the old days, people used to prepare for a typhoon by making giant crosses on their window panes using packing tape, as if to ward off evil spirits. The idea was not so much to reinforce the windows as to prevent shards of broken glass from flying into the apartment. People don't seem to bother much with that any more. Perhaps we now use better building materials, or perhaps we don't fear the wind as much because densely packed pencil buildings have dramatically reduced airflow. Instead, what worries many people about a big storm is the flying cockroach. Confused by changes in atmospheric pressure, the creepy crawlies suddenly turn airborne and dart from one end of the room to another. Giant roaches are disgusting as they are, but with wings they are what Winston Churchill would have called "the sum of all fears."

Despite our katsaridaphobia, typhoons are generally a cause for celebration in Hong Kong. They are the cultural equivalent of a snow day in America and the happiest event on the calendar after Chinese New Year. As we bemoan another never-ending work week and begrudgingly put on our work clothes on a Monday morning, we turn on the morning news and hear the magic words: "T8 is hoisted." It is second only to winning the lottery in making a Hong Konger jump for joy. That's why we cheer on the storms as if they were Olympic athletes: faster, higher, stronger! In case we needed any proof that we are an overworked people, look no further than the way we pray for a typhoon despite the devastation it inflicts on neighboring countries.

Praying for a T8

Indeed, a typhoon day promises something for everyone. Office workers get a day's vacation. Students have their classes canceled, exams rescheduled or the dreaded sports day postponed. Thrill seekers line up along the Tsim Sha Tsui waterfront and watch 15-foot waves crash on the sea walls. Seafood lovers take their fishing gear to Aberdeen or Tseung Kwan O to catch squid, which are known to form squads in calmer waters during big storms.

No one stands to benefit from a typhoon more than taxi drivers. They pick up stranded passengers and charge them up to HK$200 (US$25) on top of the meter. The "storm surcharge" is meant to compensate cab drivers for the risk of getting into an accident, as vehicular damage during a T8 storm is not covered by auto insurance. Since the law forbids anyone from driving without third party insurance, that means cab drivers are in fact risking prison to get you home safely. All things considered, $200 is actually a bargain.

By and large, the vast majority of the population has the good sense to stay home on a typhoon day. After all, we have nowhere to go because shops and restaurants are closed; all modes of transport – buses, the MTR and ferries – are suspended. The bustling city suddenly grinds to a complete halt. If getting the flu is the way our body tells us to take a break, then typhoons would be nature's hint that we as a society should slow down once in a while. So we do exactly that. In Hong Kong, social convention dictates that there are only two appropriate activities during a typhoon: eat instant noodles and watch the news.

Instant noodles are our favorite cooked food. Every household has at least a week's supply in the kitchen cabinet, which makes them the most reliable storm companion. Once the noodles are prepared – which takes no more and no less than two minutes – we set the MSG-laced meal on the coffee table and turn on the television. We slurp and chomp while watching newscasters clad in obligatory yellow raincoats scream into the microphone. We take pleasure in seeing fellow citizens run for cover from one side of the street to another, with their umbrellas turned inside out and reduced to wire carcasses. It's the best kind of reality TV.

Nevertheless, typhoons are not always fun and games. Every few years, we get a super storm that brings more than squally rains and gusty winds. The most devastating storm in Hong Kong's history was the Great Typhoon of 1937 that killed 11,000 people. In 1960, typhoon Mary claimed 1,600 lives and left tens of thousands homeless. Although the city has come a long way in making itself more storm proof, there are always a few unlucky denizens of the city injured by fallen awnings and collapsed scaffoldings. There is also flooding in low lying areas and mudslides along the hills. Dried seafood shops on Sheung Wan's Wing Lok Street were perennial victims of typhoons and black rains until 2012 when a massive underground water system was built in the area.

Another type of economic cost is lost income. There are roughly 250 business days in a calendar year, which means that shutting down the city for a single day reduces our GDP by about 0.4%. Each day the stock market is closed, billions are lost in commissions and other transaction-based revenues. The Hong Kong Stock Exchange, of which the government is the largest shareholder, stands to lose the most as trading volume is what drives its bottom line.

The government's vested interest in keeping the corporate machine running has spawned many conspiracy theories about the Hong Kong Observatory, the government department that decides when to issue a storm signal. Many accuse it of putting dollars ahead of public safety. The Observatory has been known to delay a T8 announcement until after the stock market has closed or take down the signal early to avoid disrupting the morning commute. Sometimes it does it the other way around. The Observatory appears a bit trigger happy with the storm signals before a big anti-government protest in an attempt to discourage turnout. In Hong Kong, he who holds the anemometer makes the rules.

During the three-year period between 2004 and 2007, the Hong Kong Observatory did not issue a single T8 or black rain signal. The dry spell irked citizens and thus began a popular urban legend. It is said that Li Ka-shing, property tycoon and the richest man in Hong Kong, has invented a powerful shield to ward off typhoons and rainstorms. To keep employees at their desks, the so-called "Li's Field" is activated whenever a weather system approaches. The suggestion is preposterous, but it underscores the resentment harbored by the local population against a government seen as working in cahoots with big business. After all, if you can't laugh about it, you will just have to cry.

When the typhoon finally passes, we are left with fallen tree branches on the sidewalk and toppled flower pots on the balcony. Heavy rains will continue for a few more days before the blazing sun once again scorches the city and erases all traces of a storm. To many Hong Kongers, typhoons are welcome visitors because they give us the hope of a day off. Most importantly, they remind us of how blessed we truly are, for as much as Mother Nature enjoys unleashing her whimsical wrath on Japan, the Philippines and Indonesia, so far she has chosen to take mercy on us and pull her punches year after year.

新年、舊俗

New Year, Old Customs

To the 1.3 billion ethnic Chinese living around the globe – roughly a fifth of the world's population – the Lunar New Year is the mother of all celebrations. Cantonese people take things up a few notches and, over the centuries, have developed a suite of regimented festivities that render the Twelve Days of Christmas dull by comparison.

In Hong Kong, the sanctuary where Cantonese customs are preserved and refined, our new year tradition is a combination of Christmas (the customs of exchanging gifts and putting up a decorated tree in the living room), Thanksgiving (the all-important family dinner no matter how busy or far away we are), Halloween (the get-out-of-jail-free-card for children to gorge on unlimited candy) and, of course, the Gregorian calendar New Year (the sense of renewal that compels us to draw up a list of resolutions).

The city kicks into high gear weeks before New Year's Day. Shops, restaurants and public transport blast earsplitting holiday tunes and turn the entire city into a sea of red and gold. At home, families plaster their walls with *fai chun* (揮春), strips of paper inscribed with four character wishes of prosperity, good health and domestic harmony.

God of Fortune holding up a fai chun

As soon as the clock strikes twelve on New Year's Eve, however, the whole atmosphere changes. Anticipation and excitement give way to a heightened sense of vigilance. From that point on, every phone call is answered with "*kung hey fat choi*" (恭喜發財; literally, may you come into a windfall) instead of "hello." Brooms, mops and vacuum cleaners are laid to rest for fear of "sweeping away" good fortune. Family members big and small are held to the highest standard of verbal discipline and are forbidden from using words like "death," "misfortune," "loss" or anything that sounds like them. Violations of the gag order are punished with the dramatic interjection *choi* (哫), followed by public condemnation. To redeem himself, the offender must take it all back by spitting on the floor and rephrasing what he said without the offending word.

In Hong Kong, the new year is not the new year without the famous red packets called *lai see* (利是). The tradition started out with married couples giving young children a trifle of pocket money as a holiday treat. As kids, my brother Dan and I would compete to see who got more money – a measure of our popularity among relatives – and spend it all on new toys as soon as the spending moratorium ended on the 15th day of the new year. From time to time, my mom would tell us stories about exemplary children using *lai see* earnings to pay household bills, stories that Dan and I dismissed as a ploy to guilt us into surrendering our hard earned cash.

Today, *lai see* has lost much of its original wholesomeness and evolved into a form of socially acceptable bribery. From doormen to secretaries and restaurant greeters, anyone in a position to make our lives easier will expect a "show of appreciation" to grease the wheels for the next twelve months. The more aggressive ones will come after you and bombard you with four character wishes until you finally get the point and surrender the money.

In keeping with the season of renewal, families will loosen the purse strings and stock up on all things new: new clothes, new shoes and new appliances. Back in the 1960s and 70s when Hong Kong was still a cottage industry economy, those extra expenses were enough to create a liquidity crunch known in the local vernacular as *nin kwan* (年關; literally, the new year trial). The financial bind was further exacerbated by the customs of *bai nin* (拜年; literally, the new year visit), when friends and family would go to each other's homes during the first week of the year. Personal hardship notwithstanding, visitors bore generous gifts, put on their smartest clothes and looked cheerful when they presented themselves to the hosts. Nowadays, higher disposable incomes mean few of us would wait until the new year to buy new things, and fewer still would feel the need to parade well-groomed children once a year to create an illusion of abundance. Chinese New Year is a much less stressful event than it used to be.

As is the case for most Chinese festivals, food figures prominently in the New Year celebration. Cantonese people fill their kitchens with turnip cakes, tarot cakes and *nin go* (年糕) made from glutinous rice, cane sugar and lard. As a child I used to watch my mom roll up her sleeves to prepare homemade *tong yuen* (湯圓; glutinous rice balls) from scratch. She would tell me that she learned the recipe from her mom, who had learned it from her mom, my great grandmother. Alas, the tradition of passing down holiday food recipes ended with my generation. In this day and age, no one seems to have the patience to mix, knead, roll and steam when we can walk into any local dessert place and purchase a bowl of *tong yuen* at HK$15 (US$2).

One of the most exciting new year festivities is the flower market, a week long bazaar with hundreds of booths selling seasonal flowers and toys. It has in recent years become a training ground for young entrepreneurs wishing to sell trinkets they design and produce. The Victoria Park markets, the biggest in the city, draw hundreds of thousands of visitors each year and turn the half dozen contiguous soccer fields into the equivalent of New York's Times Square on New Year's Eve. Back in the day, getting lost in the dizzying crowds was a nightmare scenario for parents and kids alike. So the whole family stuck together, hand-in-hand, and walked through aisle upon aisle of daffodils, gladiolas and cherry trees.

For children, the bazaar was the one place they could forget their good manners and demand new toys. I will never forget the first remote control car my dad bought me at the flower market when I was four. Two hours of non-stop nagging, stomping and sulking had finally paid off. But since kids nowadays get showered with toys all year around, going to the bazaar is more an annual ritual than a shopping trip to which they look forward. What's more, because everyone has a cell phone, family members often split up as soon as they arrive at the market and meet back at an appointed exit when they are ready to leave.

No matter how much things have changed, Chinese New Year will always be the most important time of the year in Hong Kong. As the city grows more affluent, however, an annual event to give thanks to what we have and to wish for what we don't is becoming less and less relevant. All the magic and romance associated with the festival, the pain and joy of getting through another year, seem to increasingly elude the younger generations. I worry that Chinese New Year will one day become a set of customs we follow but no longer understand. When it comes to tradition and culture, it seems, a higher standard of living can be a mixed blessing.

服
務
為
先 **Are You Being Served?**

I had been sitting at my table for 15 minutes, with neither a menu nor a glass of water. For the fifth time I put up my hand and waved at the waitress who pretended she hadn't seen me. When our eyes finally met, I gave her a big smile and mouthed the word *carte*. She gritted her teeth and said: "*Monsieur, je n'ai que deux mains.*" Translation: "I only have two hands."

To many frequent travelers to Europe, my rather unpleasant dining experience at the Parisian restaurant is all too familiar. From store clerks in Rome to bus drivers in Geneva and airport security in London, customer service personnel in Europe are trained to be rude. The situation is particularly egregious in France because you are expected to speak their language and they are protected by permissive labor law and powerful unions. What's more, bad service nearly always goes hand-in-hand with inefficiency. Whether you are checking into a hotel or getting a tax refund at the airport, everything takes twice as long and is ten times harder in Europe. Moss grows on your feet before you are summoned by a person who acts like a prankster on *Candid Camera*. If you don't believe me, try opening a bank account in The Netherlands and you'll get the idea. When the European debt crisis hit a few years ago, as Germany and France scrambled to bail out Greece and Portugal while Spain and Italy teetered on the brink of a recession, I wondered whether their reckoning was a long time coming.

Service without a smile

For all its rich culture, high fashion and breathtaking landscapes, Europe is decades behind the rest of the industrialized world in customer service. My European friends, especially those who have lived in Asia for a number of years, would be the first to agree. One of the main reasons is the very thing that makes Europe a great place: egalitarianism. In Europe, the server demands as much respect as the one being served, which explains why the waiter has no qualms saying "Can't you see I'm busy?" And because people in the service industry treat you like one of their own, they see nothing wrong in telling you "I only have two hands!"

On the other side of the Atlantic one observes a very different scene. In America, as the cliché goes, the customer is always right. From Olive Garden to the Cheesecake Factory, a bubbly waitress will usher you to your table, get on one knee to take your order and check on you throughout the meal with a smiley "How's everything today?" And yes, her name is Katie and you can just holler if you need another refill on that soda. Change your mind about those GAP jeans? Bring them back within 90 days for a full refund. You don't even need a receipt. Unhappy with the service? Ask to speak to the supervisor and receive a coupon in appreciation of your valuable feedback. Try doing the same in Italy and all you get is a dry laugh or an obscene gesture.

But nothing is actually free in the Land of the Free. Tipping is a big part of the service industry. How much to tip and when to do it are questions that can trip up even the most seasoned of travelers. In New York, for instance, a 15% gratuity at restaurants is just a starting point, a bare minimum. When you check into a hotel, the going rate for taking your luggage to the room is US$5 (HK$40) per piece. I've had a bellboy standing in my room with his hand outstretched asking, "Where is my tip?" Then there are the taxi drivers, the doormen, the coat check ladies and the restroom attendants. Leave Katie a 10% tip and she will run after you and ask what she did wrong. It is expensive to be a customer in America; and being always right carries a hefty price.

When it comes to customer service, there is no place like Asia. Asian airlines, hotels and airports are consistently rated the best in the world. Service staff in this part of the world, especially those in Japan and Thailand, bend over backwards to accommodate the customer. They rarely expect a tip and will never ask for one. Surely there are exceptions. A weekend in Shanghai, the wealthiest city in China, will provide ample evidence that customer service is a state of mind that takes years to develop. It doesn't happen overnight no matter how much money you throw at it. The waitresses at the *über chic* Park Hyatt Shanghai are all smiles, but ask for a vegetarian menu and they get confused and recommend the chicken salad.

In Hong Kong, the service industry has seen remarkable progress since the city came of age in the 1970s. It wasn't too long ago when bank tellers yelled at customers for not filling out a deposit form properly. Since the government's famous advertising campaign starring celebrity Andy Lau to promote quality customer service, however, the hospitality industry as a whole has undergone a cultural revolution. One of the first things that hit me when I moved back to Hong Kong was how far the city's service industry has come. When the cashier at 7-Eleven handed me my change and said, "Thank you, please come again," I got a little misty-eyed.

In the last decade, the surging influx of mainland Chinese visitors – some of them can be rough around the edges – has put a strain on the service industry. Restaurant staff and store clerks in Hong Kong are known to respond in kind, ordering their Mandarin-speaking customers to *deng yi xia* (wait a moment) and *qing pai dui* (get in line) without so much of a smile or eye contact. In the zero-sum game of customer service, the mistreatment of one group has raised the status of another: native Hong Kongers who speak and behave just like the people who serve him. As soon as one walks through the door, he will be greeted with a look of relief. And when he opens his mouth and out comes crisp, accent-free Cantonese – a Masonic handshake of sorts, he might even be let in on a special promotion kept secret from the outgroup.

Every time I travel outside of Asia, I am reminded how spoiled I am to live in this part of the world. For all the things we complain about in Hong Kong, it only takes a trip abroad to realize how good we have it. Whether we are making a dinner reservation, asking for directions at the MTR or even disputing our tax bill with the government, service people in Hong Kong are courteous, efficient and professional. I went to school in Europe and travel there frequently for both work and pleasure. I simply can't imagine living there and having to deal with the *je m'en fiche* ("I don't care") mentality on a daily basis. French hills and Greek islands, no matter how charming, will not lower my blood pressure.

別人的派對 Someone Else's Party

Late March in Hong Kong brings clammy air, frequent drizzles and the gradual return of the subtropical heat. It is also marked by a spike in beer consumption and hotel room rates, caused not by the arrival of spring but a spectacle known as the Hong Kong Sevens. The three day rugby tournament is much more than just an international sporting event. To expatriates living in Hong Kong, it is a celebration bigger than Christmas and New Year. It is a cross between the Super Bowl, Halloween and Oktoberfest. It is Mardi Gras without the parade and Spring Break with bam bam sticks. The annual carnival fills the Hong Kong Stadium with cheers, beer breath and spontaneous eruptions of song and dance.

They get really into it

Rugby sevens, as the name would suggest, involves fewer players than regular rugby. Each game consists merely of two seven-minute halves. Think of it as beach volleyball or five-a-side soccer. To prove that size doesn't matter, rugby sevens made its Olympic debut at the 2016 Summer Games in Rio de Janeiro.

The first Hong Kong Sevens tournament was held in 1976. The sport was introduced to the British colony by a handful of rugby-loving English businessmen. Securing Cathay Pacific as a corporate sponsor ensured the event's survival in an otherwise unathletic city. Indeed, the lack of local participation has always been a public relations issue for the Sevens. There wasn't a single ethnic Chinese on the local team until Fuk-Ping Chan became the first Hong Kong born player to represent the city in 1997. Even today, the "Hong Kong Dragons" look more like the starting lineup of Manchester United than their parochial team name would suggest.

Rugby is a decidedly English pastime. The sport is dominated by Commonwealth nations around the world. England and ex-British colonies like Australia, New Zealand, Fiji and Samoa are favorites at the Hong Kong Sevens, which is why thousands of Brits, Aussies and Kiwis living in Hong Kong flock to the games every year. It didn't take long before Americans and expats from other non-rugby-playing countries took notice. Rugby fans or not, they jumped on the bandwagon and turned the event into a pan-Caucasian extravaganza. During the Sevens weekend, expats and tourists swamp the Hong Kong Stadium and overrun restaurants and bars nearby. The normally quiet Caroline Hill Road in Causeway Bay – the only entry point to the stadium – is packed to the hilt. Streets are cordoned off for crowd control and scalpers are everywhere. Unhired taxis become the hottest commodity in town. The south stand of the stadium is where the rowdiest crowds congregate and minors are denied entry for safety reasons, which also makes it the most exciting place to be in Hong Kong.

Despite all the hullabaloo, the Hong Kong Sevens is a non-event among the locals. Unlike the Standard Chartered Marathon or the Stanley Dragon Boat Championships – both of which draw large local crowds – the Sevens is irrelevant to 95% of the city's population and receives little to no coverage from the Chinese press. If it weren't for the backed up traffic in Causeway Bay during that weekend, most locals wouldn't even know that there was a tournament happening. For three days in March, the Hong Kong Stadium is a sea of *gweilo* holding a beer in one hand and a hot dog in the other. It is as odd as going to the French Open and finding the Roland Garros Stadium full of, say, Japanese faces. If you look hard enough, you may spot the occasional local Hong

Konger trying to blend in. To the average rugby-indifferent local, the Sevens is nothing but a tourist trap designed by businesses to promote air travel and boost hotel occupancy. With all the money visitors splurge on tickets, food, accommodation and official merchandise, the Hong Kong Sevens is easily the city's biggest weekend in terms of tourism dollars.

The Sevens' failure to catch on with the local population has as much to do with the sport's limited popularity as it does with access. The increasing commercialization of the event is shutting out people outside the rugby-playing or finance community. Out of the 40,000 tickets to the tournament, less than 10% are available to the general public through an online lottery. The rest of them are either reserved for rugby clubs or sold in large blocks to corporations.

Inside the stadium, much of the east and west stands are converted into "by invitation only" corporate boxes. The arrangement allows bankers and lawyers to entertain valued clients in what has become the most important marketing event on the calendar. How many tickets a given client receives and whether he ends up on the main stand or in an upper level executive suite depends on the amount of business he has given the host in the past year. It is nothing personal. If you don't work in finance or know someone who does, on the other hand, good luck with the lottery. The chance of winning it is less than one in ten.

As a child growing up in Hong Kong, I never heard of the Sevens. But since I moved back to the city a few years ago, I have gone to the event every year. Although I enjoy neither rugby nor beer, and much less dressing up in a superhero costume, I make a point of going if only for a few hours. Like the rest of the people in the stadium, I gorge on bad ballpark food, dodge spilled beer and queue up outside overcrowded toilets. I pay little attention to the games and know close to nothing about the rules. Instead, I say hello to my friends, exchange a few business cards and pick up the latest gossip in the banking circles. It is a check-the-box exercise I don't mind doing. The glaring absence of locals, whether by choice or by circumstance, still bothers me. Nevertheless, each time I see what a genuinely good time everyone is having, I say to myself: Why not? They only get to do this once a year.

Dining Out...

I

The Michelin Guide published its first Hong Kong/Macau edition in 2011. Since then, the little red book has sparked spirited debate and sometimes even nationalistic rumblings among citizens. Hong Kongers balk at the idea of a bunch of foreigners judging our food, when most of the undercover inspectors sent by the guide can't tell a fish maw from a fish belly or know the first thing about *dun* (燉), *mun* (焖), *zing* (蒸), *pou* (泡) and *zoek* (灼) – to name but a few ways a Chinese chef may cook his ingredients with steam. For many of us, it seems far wiser to spend the HK$200 (US$25, that's how much the guide costs) on a couple of hairy crabs than on a restaurant directory published by a tire manufacturer.

Food is a tricky business. It confounds even the most sophisticated of cultures and peoples. The English and the Germans, for instance, excel in everything else except for the one thing that matters most. Young nations like America, Australia and Canada have yet to make a name for themselves in the culinary world. They must pay their dues by sending their best chefs overseas to study other people's food. By contrast, countries blessed with rich culinary histories hold up their cooking traditions as a testament to their superiority. People from these proud nations cannot stop telling the stories behind popular dishes. They are simultaneously offended and flattered by copycat cuisines and consider fusion a form of pollution.

Of all the worthy cuisines out there, French and Chinese are the reigning champions. Sure, Koreans have their *gogi gui*, Spaniards their *paella* and Moroccans their lamb *tajine*. Nevertheless, when it comes to diversity, complexity and subtlety, the French and the Chinese know few competitors. Only the most ingenious and daring cooks would, for instance, think of putting frogs, snakes, brains and tripe on the menu and pull it off brilliantly. No other language rivals French and Chinese in having a rich vocabulary devoted to food and food preparation. For centuries, European royalty checked their egos at the palace door and staffed their imperial kitchens with armies of French chefs. Even today, heads of state across South East Asia regale dignitaries with nothing but Chinese food at state events.

Trailing behind the French and the Chinese are the Japanese. The distant third boasts dishes made with fresh seasonal ingredients and arranged in stunning, museum worthy presentations. The edible art of Japanese cooking is best showcased by *kaiseki* (懷石料理), a multi-course affair featuring a menu that smacks of a wedding rhyme:

Something steamed (蒸物), something boiled (煮物)
Something deep fried (油物), something broiled (焼物)
And a lacquered tray with a gold foil

Daniel Boulud, a three-star celebrity chef from France

Once you get past the intricate presentation and the fancy names, however, Japanese dishes taste surprisingly ordinary. In fact, many Chinese people in my parents' generation still regard Japanese food as bland, unsophisticated and, with too much emphasis on tofu, seaweed and other humble ingredients, indicative of something created by poor peasants.

Then there is Italian, surely the world's most overrated food. The problem has nothing to do with Italy and everything to do with the Europhiles on the other side of the Atlantic. Obsessed with all things Italian, Americans romanticize the mafia, go gaga over the Sicilian accent, and hype up Italian cooking to *haute cuisine* status. Mention Italian food anywhere in America and people give you words like "high end," "exclusive" and "refined." Over the years, this manmade culinary phenomenon spread to the rest of the world like a disease. From Buenos Aires and Berlin to Shanghai and Singapore, hoity-toity Italian restaurants lure gullible patrons with trite opera tunes and charge exorbitant prices for everyday foods.

No matter how much they window-dress it, pasta and risotto are starchy foods that the French regard merely as side dishes and the Chinese use as stomach fillers at the end of a banquet meal. And no matter how much Mario Batali and Rocco DiSpirito like to say every Italian word with an overdone accent or brag about their travels in Tuscany in search of secret recipes, ossobuco and chicken marsala are never as sophisticated as what these celebrity chefs would have you believe. So let me set the record straight once and for all: Italian cooking is about being hearty and folksy, not panache and refinement.

Don't get me wrong – I love Italian food and I cook it every chance I get. During my boarding school years in Trieste, an idyllic city perched on the Adriatic coast in northeastern Italy, I spent many evenings with local families gorging on homemade gnocchi and polenta and many more nights in the dormitory kitchen preparing *al dente* pasta with nothing but olive oil and garlic. That's when I tasted Italian cooking at its best, not at some five-star restaurant, but at a cozy dinner party where the main ingredients were cheers and laughs. Those fond memories rush back whenever I sauté fresh basil in a buttered skillet or watch the steam rise from the sink when draining a pot of boiled spaghetti.

Food is an art form as subjective as any other. Perhaps comparing Italian and Japanese cooking to French and Chinese cuisines is no more meaningful than pitting Beijing opera against a Gregorian chant, or the Taj Mahal against the Chateau de Versailles. Perhaps good food has much more to do with our life experience and the memories we associate it with, than exotic ingredients and elaborate preparation. And perhaps I am amiss for not mentioning other fine cuisines such as Indian, Thai and Mexican. All that highlights what an impossible feat *The Michelin Guide* has undertaken by making a foray into the Hong Kong restaurant scene.

II

Both my freelance work and my day job give me plenty of opportunities to live out a foodie's dream. As a restaurant reviewer I get to try out fancy new places and sample their best dishes for free. The price to pay, however, is having to keep detailed notes of everything I put in my mouth so that I can spit out a thousand words on a two-page magazine spread the next day. Likewise, expensing client lunches sounds like a no-lose proposition until I find myself stuck with a table of stodgy bankers yapping about China's next big IPO and why everyone should buy gold. It all bears out the old adage that there is no such thing as a free lunch.

Hong Kong is an epicurean paradise and we have the numbers to prove it. There are over 40,000 eating establishments listed on *Open Rice*, the city's popular online restaurant guide. Based on that figure alone and excluding thousands of hole-in-the-wall noodle houses and neighborhood kitchens yet to be catalogued by the website, our restaurants per capita is nearly twice as high as New York City or London.

Navigating the city's hyperactive restaurant scene can be daunting. Friends and colleagues often come to me for recommendations when planning a birthday or anniversary dinner. One question I get asked a lot is what my favorite restaurants are in Hong Kong. In terms of service, ambience and food – the three categories by which food critics score a restaurant – my top picks are the legendary Mandarin Grill, David Tang's retro-chic China Club and Toscana under the helm of executive chef Umberto Bombana. Unfortunately for us, Toscana closed shop several years ago when the Ritz Carlton Hotel on Chater Road was demolished. Mr. Bombana's subsequent ventures have never quite measured up to his past success.

For every Mandarin Grill, China Club and Toscana in the city, there are thousands of restaurants that fall short in terms of service and ambience. Let's begin with service. Many restaurants here operate under the misguided notion that quality of service is measured by how quickly dishes are cleared from the table. Fast eaters, with their plates taken away as soon as they finish eating, must sit in front of an empty placemat and watch their friends eat the rest of their meal. In more extreme cases, diners find themselves in a tug-of-war with an overzealous waiter, while that last strand of pasta dangles precariously between their mouth and the vanishing plate, dripping sauce and all.

Anyone in the restaurant business will tell you that nothing annoys customers more than tardy food arrivals. People get cranky when they are hungry – it's called hypoglycemia. Unless you are ordering a Peking duck or a chocolate soufflé, your food should arrive within 20 minutes, tops. Anything past that point warrants a polite follow-up with your server. As if restaurant staff in Hong Kong were all taught to lie, however, every request to check on a late order is invariably hit back with a robotic smile and a patronizing "It's on its way, sir." How the waiter can offer that assurance without so much as a trip to the kitchen will baffle you until you chase again, only to discover that your order was never placed. "Do you still want it, sir?" he asks with the same robotic smile.

With the exception of restaurants in hotels, shopping malls and dining enclaves like SoHo and Star Street, eateries in Hong Kong generally pay very little attention to their décor. The wisdom that "you eat with your eyes first" has yet to gain traction in our city. As a result, décor can range from poor taste to downright revolting. Wet floor, sticky floor. Dirty carpeting and peeling wallpaper. A *guan gung* (關公; a Taoist deity) shrine next to a giant television. Customers queuing outside washrooms reeking of chlorine masking more unpleasant odors. Thankfully, restaurant groups like Maxim's, which began buying up local restaurants in the 1980s, have introduced more uniform standards in restaurant management, providing safe harbors for those with a low tolerance for poor ambience and hygiene.

My gripe about service and décor notwithstanding, the quality of food in Hong Kong is generally very high. No matter where you go and how much you pay, it is difficult to get bad food in a restaurant. Whereas fierce competition and instant feedback on the Internet have weeded out most bad apples, modern technology has made preparing good food easier than ever. Gone are the days when you had to travel to Sham Tseng (深井) for that perfectly roasted squab or Lei Yue Mun (鯉魚門) for the best steamed grouper in town. Nowadays any restaurant with an electronic steamer or broiler can cook those same dishes just as well. That's good news for the seven million hungry citizens but very bad news for venerable names like Yung Kee (鏞記), Luk Yu (陸羽) and Mak An Kee (麥奀記). Once the sole guardians of culinary secrets, these big names with an overpriced menu have all but lost their allure and must rely on unwary tourists and a dwindling base of regulars to keep them afloat.

Yung Kee on Wellington Street, best known for its roast goose

When it comes to eating out, Hong Kongers are spoiled for choice and spoiled for price. For a fraction of what we have to pay in other major cities, we get to feast on world class restaurant food day in and day out. What's more, if Cantonese cooking is the most sophisticated among all regional varieties of Chinese cuisine, then Hong Kong being the Cantonese food capital of the world makes us some of luckiest people around. Nevertheless, our rich culinary culture can be too much of a good thing. From Sichuan and Hunan specialties to Italian risotto and Japanese teppanyaki, regional and international cuisines can't escape a bit of "Cantonization" to pander to the local palate, resulting in everything tasting more or less like, well, Cantonese food. That's the price we all must pay for having affordable, delicious food anywhere, any time. Didn't I tell you there is no free lunch?

...Or Eating In

I

New Yorkers often joke about keeping their sweaters in the oven because they never cook. Hong Kongers would have loved to do the same, if only we had the space for an oven. The lack of a proper kitchen and the ease of dining out have made home cooking a vanishing art in the city. At times it seems like no one around us – other than those penny pinching, foldable cart pushing *see lai* (師奶; middle-aged housewives) – bothers to prepare a home cooked meal any more.

Cooking is time consuming. Considering that most worker bees get home just before the 9:30 soap opera starts, banging and clanging in the kitchen is the last thing on their minds. From buying groceries to all that washing, chopping, frying and steaming, the whole production is guaranteed to take up the entire evening – time better spent slumping in front of the television with a bucket of fried chicken. That doesn't even include the time to do dishes, a chore so universally hated that marriages have been broken and children disowned over it.

Cooking is also expensive. Because few of us step into the kitchen much these days, when we finally decide to deign ourselves to cook something, it is often for a special occasion and accompanied with fanfare. Refusing to rough it with second grade ingredients, we turn to City Super, ThreeSixty and other gourmet grocery stores in the city. There, organic vegetables and prized meats are arranged in irresistible displays and tagged with eye-popping prices, not to mention the thousands of food miles they have logged having been flown in from Australia and The Netherlands. Even in more affordable supermarkets like Wellcome and Park'n Shop, rising food prices in China – the main source of our fresh produce – have pushed up the cost of cooking, making that takeout flyer from the neighborhood Cantonese restaurant all the more enticing.

Then there is the space issue. As a child I developed a mild phobia of the kitchen. The crammed space in our Tin Hau apartment was stuffy, greasy and fraught with peril. Scorching hot appliances, dripping condiment containers, window bars coated with grime, and the most frightening of all, dark crevices where tiny morsels of food were trapped and that devil's own creation – the giant cockroach – lurked at all hours of the day. Growing up I always thought my mother was a brave woman for slaving away in the punishing room churning out meal after meal for a family of seven.

Any real estate agent in the city will tell you that the newer the building the smaller the kitchen gets. For many local homes, it is a 15-square-foot telephone booth big enough to fit only one person. What is meant to be the center of family life has degenerated into a glorified pantry where one does little more than boil water and cook instant noodles. The two-door refrigerator, the largest of all household appliances, is often expelled from the kitchen and banished to a lonely corner in the living room. It is one of the unique features of a true Hong Kong home.

Cooking is a sexy skill

Either by choice or by circumstance, few people in Hong Kong get to experience the joy of cooking. In a city where time is money and space is gold, this critical life skill, a symbol of self-reliance, has fallen by the wayside. In the process we have also lost a powerful weapon in our social arsenal. While anyone can impress a loved one with flowers or jewelry – as we often do in a consumer-driven city – it is he who takes the trouble to study a recipe, practice it days in advance and whip up a feast that wins the heart. By the end of the evening, as the date praises the perfectly grilled steaks and candlelight flickers against a pair of empty glasses, the cook with the silly apron is certain to get a lot more than just a kiss. If that's not enough incentive to pick up cooking, I don't know what is.

II

In many parts of the world, dinner parties are a time honored tradition. Self-respecting men and women open up their homes to regale friends with home-cooked food and stimulating conversation. The cultural significance of these gatherings is evidenced by the prominent role they play in literature and films. In *Mrs. Dalloway*, Virginia Woolf devotes an entire book to describing a house party. In the 1967 classic *Guess Who's Coming to Dinner*, the taboo subject of interracial marriage is dealt with at one of Hollywood's most memorable suppers.

Dinner parties are also a source of endless intrigue. They provide the perfect setting for a "whodunit" murder mystery, as they do in Agatha Christie's *Thirteen at Dinner*, Alfred Hitchcock's *Rope* and more recently in *Gosford Park*. The tradition has even made it to the list of most frequently asked questions at job interviews: If you were hosting a dinner and could invite three people, dead or alive, who would you choose?

In North America and much of Europe, a person's first dinner party signifies his rite of passage into full adulthood. To pull it off, the host needs self-confidence, creativity and an eagle's eye for detail. If he looks a bit nervous, that's because his reputation is on the line. He knows too well that when guests admire his book collection and inquire about the origin of every piece of furniture, they are taking mental notes about his taste and social standing. So before every housewarming dinner, Thanksgiving feast or Oscar party, stressed out hosts find themselves buzzing around the house, hiding their boy band music collection and replacing *Entertainment Weekly* with *The Economist* on the coffee table. Lava lamps and action figures are removed to make way for scented candles and crystal stemware.

While dinner parties are a way of life in the West, they are not nearly as common in Asia. It is possible that Asian people feel squeamish about revealing too much about their private lives. It is also possible that the family unit is so tight it leaves little room for prying friends. Considering that many young adults live with their parents until they get married, things can get a little awkward with mom and dad staring at guests and cramping their style all night long.

In Hong Kong, people rarely cook and they never entertain. The space issue alone is enough reason to rule out the living room as a venue for social gatherings. That's why everyone meets in public places like restaurants, shopping malls and karaoke bars. Chinese New Year is the only time when friends and relatives break the rule and visit each other's home bearing butter cookies and *lai see*. Even this once-a-year tradition is slowly vanishing, as most people under the age of 50 are eager to skip it and go to the movies instead.

Privacy and space alone, however, do not explain why we haven't embraced the custom of entertaining. Another key factor is the requirement to cook. The availability of cheap domestic help has stripped an entire generation of their domestic skills, from preparing a proper meal to doing laundry or fixing the toilet flush. We no longer set foot in the kitchen except to check on the maid. Hand someone a turnip or salmon fillet and he will look at you sideways and ask, "What am I supposed to do with this?" Because one of the main goals of hosting is to show off the gastrosexual's culinary skills, those who lack them prefer to save themselves the embarrassment. After all, ordering a pizza delivery or having the maid cater a party is considered very bad form.

As much as we are reluctant hosts, we are also reluctant guests. To most people in Hong Kong, attending a house party – typically hosted by an overzealous Western coworker – is more of a chore than a privilege. The evening always ends up being a lot of work, with all that polite chitchat about art, foreign cinema, or, the deadliest of all topics, sports. For those who don't really follow world news or haven't read a book since college graduation, contribution to any intellectual conversation is limited to "Hmm, that's interesting." Worse still, dinner parties are usually "plus one" events and we have to drag our reluctant spouse along for five never-ending hours of nodding, smiling and, once in a while, a peal of fake belly laughs.

For years, I have been on a one man crusade to lift the Asian embargo on dinner parties. I host one at my home every few weeks. Taking into account the various cultural factors at play, I adopt a different strategy depending on the type of guests I invite. Young people, for instance, need to be stimulated at all times and so I bring out the board games and playing cards. Coworkers often prefer theme parties and so I organize wine tastings and trivia nights. Family and close friends require the least amount of work. I simply stock up on wine and let the conversation take us wherever it may. As a general policy, I keep my "circles" separate because mixing them together, based on firsthand experience, doesn't usually work.

Having hosted dozens of dinners over the years, I am no stranger to the many odd party behaviors in Hong Kong. I have watched guests go through my fridge and pantry (without asking) scouring for snacks. Some jam to their own music from their iPhones, while others sit in the corner playing the video games they bring. Still others show up with ice-cream when I have asked them to bring ice for the cocktails. I once had a young lady arrive at 10:30pm with three uninvited companions, all demanding to be fed. And because the road to hell is paved with good intentions, an occasional well intended guest will bring his own food and turn my carefully planned three-course dinner into a potluck. These are all true stories, the kind that would make etiquette queen Emily Post roll over in her grave.

No party *faux pas* is more frustrating than the television phenomenon. Prime time programming is such an indispensable part of our evening routine that some of us are lost without it. The television is the first thing we turn on when we get home, and the last thing we switch off before we go to bed. If you stand outside a local home at 8pm on any given night, you will hear family conversation interlaced with dramatic soap opera dialogue. These are the unmistakable sounds of Hong Kong homes after dark. As a host, I have grown used to guests asking me to have the television switched on during dinner. The more determined ones will grab the remote control and turn on the television themselves. When challenged, they will look me in the eye and ask, "No TV? What are we supposed to do all night?"

To prove that I don't only pick on my own kind, I should point out that other cultures have their party oddities too. For instance, people in Spain don't start serving dinner until as late as 10pm. In Venezuela, the guests send flowers, usually orchids, to the host in advance of the party. When it comes to social quirks, the English are the ones to beat. I haven't met an Englishman (or woman) who isn't obsessed with serving hot beverages. A typical English household is a mini-Fortnum & Mason store, where a selection of peppermint, Earl Grey and Darjeeling teabags lie *mise en place* on the kitchen counter.

"Tea is the appropriate response to every situation in life," my English friend Louise explains. "I could have just told the hostess that my father had passed away or that I was getting a divorce. Whatever the circumstance is, she will immediately disappear into the kitchen to fix me a cup of tea, leaving me weeping alone on the sofa. I may be inconsolable, but that doesn't stop her from screaming at the top of her lungs: 'MILK AND SUGAR?!'"

Suddenly, turning on the television doesn't seem so strange any more.

Pirates and Hidden Treasures

Six miles off the southwestern coast of Hong Kong Island is a piece of rock smaller than New York's Central Park. Shaped like a dumbbell, Cheung Chau – or literally Long Island in Cantonese – was once a strategic hideout for ferocious pirates who ruled the Canton coasts. At the turn of the 19th Century, these pirates of the South China Sea, our own Jack Sparrow and Captain Hook, terrorized seafarers and threatened the Qing court. The most prominent of them all, Cheung Po Tsai (張保仔), famously bisexual and captain of a vast and formidable fleet, was a staple among local legends. With all the eye makeup and flailing hand gestures, Johnny Depp might have had a certain Chinese pirate in mind when he crafted his character.

*   *   *

Cheung Po Tsai was only 21 years old when he took over the pirating business from his adoptive parents. During the short period between 1807 and 1810 – the year he capitulated to the Qing court and became an imperial navy colonel, Cheung pillaged and plundered towns and villages along the Canton coastal area, including Hong Kong and Macau. At the pinnacle of his pirating career, Cheung commanded a fleet of 600 ships and a private army of 40,000 men. Recognizing Hong Kong's strategic value to his growing enterprise, the sea lord established outposts in Stanley, Chung Hom Kok, Lantau Island and Cheung Chau.

In the eyes of the Qing court, piracy threatened not only lucrative trade channels but also the delicate relations with foreign powers. Fearing Cheung's ferocious Red Flag Clan (紅旗幫), authorities turned to the warships and cannons of the Portuguese and British navies. Nevertheless, Cheung's sea savvy and firepower allowed him to out-maneuver the coalition forces at every turn. Whenever the pirates were pushed back by their pursuers, they sought refuge in the nooks and crannies along the South China Coast. The Cheung Po Tsai Cave on the southwestern tip of Cheung Chau is one of the more famous hiding places that remains intact and is now a popular spot for treasure hunters in search of hidden fortunes.

From the son of a penniless Cantonese fisherman to the reigning chief of one of the biggest pirate clans, Cheung Po Tsai had a colorful personal life to match his professional achievements. He was just 15 when he was abducted by the notorious pirate Cheng Yat (鄭一) and his wife Lady Cheng, a former prostitute. The childless couple formally adopted Cheung as their son, but it was believed that Cheng Yat kept the teenage boy, a veritable Adonis, as his lover. Their love affair went on for six years until Cheng Yat drowned in a typhoon in 1807. After his lover's untimely death, young Cheung transferred his love to the widowed wife and married Lady Cheng, his adoptive mother. The complicated love triangle, unconventional and bold even by today's standards, allowed Cheung Po Tsai to inherit the family fortune and eventually take over the Red Flag Clan. As it were, the young pirate owed his meteoric rise in the underworld of piracy to his pursuit of free love and disdain for social norms.

*   *   *

Two weeks ago, my brothers and I decided to take the 30-minute ferry ride for a two-day getaway in Cheung Chau. The island has long been a favorite "staycation" destination among citizens who are tired of airport checkpoints and crowded flights. With a thriving population of 23,000, it is one of the few outlying islands in Hong Kong still able to sustain an active local community. There are no double-decker buses, no taxis and no motor vehicles of any sort, save for a few miniature ambulances and police cars specially made to zoom through narrow alleyways. On the crowded yet serene island, close your eyes and all you will hear are bicycle bells and restaurant crockery. Up the hill and down the street, flare your nose and you will smell nothing but sea brine, barbequed squid and burning incense. City slickers arriving by the boatload will invariably ask themselves one simple question: Could I retire here?

My brothers and I tottered off the wobbling ferry and were immediately greeted by a line of street vendors offering village lodgings and local snacks. Like a time capsule, Cheung Chau has preserved bits and pieces of Hong Kong's postwar city life. Everywhere on the island, we saw men of all ages sitting on the sidewalk chatting about nothing and everything. Children on their rusty bicycles chased stray dogs from one end of the island to the other. Along the shoreline, fishermen dried their daily catch on wicker trays in the blazing sun, while the piercing sounds of Cantonese opera blasted from a distant radio.

Taking refuge from the summer heat, I walked into a mom-and-pop *zaap for po* (雜貨鋪; general store) looking for a straw hat. The shopkeeper disappeared into the back of the store and reemerged a minute later with a half-dozen designs. After a long, unrushed process of deliberation, I walked out with a fedora for all of HK$32 (US$4). Thanks to its relative isolation from the urban population, Cheung Chau has been spared the scourge of gentrification. As a result, stores and restaurants on the island still operate under much the same business model as they did in the 1950s and 60s. Without greedy landlords raising their rent every few years, shop owners can stock more creatively and sell less aggressively. Elsewhere in the city, however, the term "general store" has all but disappeared from the retail lexicon.

After finishing lunch at a local seafood restaurant, we walked half a mile to a rental shop where we each got a bicycle to seek out the island's many sights. Apart from the famous Cheung Po Tsai Cave, a dozen quaint temples dedicated to various Taoist deities dot the island. Still, Cheung Chau is perhaps best known for the Tai Ping Tsing Chiu (太平清醮) celebrations, once a ritual to ward off plagues and now an annual festival in May that attracts tourists by the thousands. The festivities culminate with an eye-popping parade of children dressed up as folk heroes while balancing on a pole, and end with a heart-stopping series of bun snatching contests (搶包山) held at midnight.

Besides these time-honored traditions, Cheung Chau has earned a rather curious reputation among Hong Kongers. The island has long been the venue of choice for young boys and girls to lose their virginity. As part of the best (or worst) kept secret in the city, teenagers will ask for permission to have a sleepover on the island with "school friends," and unsuspecting parents will unwittingly agree. After a day of wholesome bicycling and beach volleyball, hordes of hormone raging adolescents check into affordable no-tell hotels, wash down peanuts and potato chips with a six-pack of Tsing Tao beer and lose themselves in a night of sexual free-for-all. Even though teenage intimacy is almost guaranteed to be disappointing – or should I say anticlimactic – it is a rite of passage that, if not for Cheung Chau, would have been deferred to a later stage in life and become all the more traumatic.

Highlight of the Tai Ping Tsing Chiu festivities

From my room in the Warwick Hotel on the island's East Bay, I watched moonlit waves crash on the darkened beach. At the other end of the ocean, clusters of night lights in faraway Cyberport and Lamma Island twinkled like shimmering purple stars. In the depth of a late summer's night, the sounds of bicycle bells had given way to the whispers of breaking waves and chatter of crickets. Struck by the island's serenity and charm of a bygone era, I came to realize that the real treasures of Cheung Chau are found not in ancient caves but in its laid back, understated way of life. And while the legacy of Asia's most famous pirate might have been his ferocity, it is his freewheeling spirit toward love and relationships that inspires today's youth to welcome adulthood with a sense of adventure. It is surprising that Walt Disney Pictures hasn't yet made a movie about Cheung Po Tsai. Then again, I think it already has.

History in Our Midst

A stone's throw from the din and clamor of Central, within earshot of the noisy Graham Street wet markets, is one of the city's most storied neighborhoods. Sheung Wan is a pearl lodged between the jagged shells of a concrete jungle. Each day, crowds stream through the warren of back streets but few give another thought to the treasure trove of history we have in our midst. So much of what Hong Kong is known for – trading, banking and its reputation as a global financial center – began there. Contrary to what the guidebook says, the area is much more than just antiques and dried seafood.

* * *

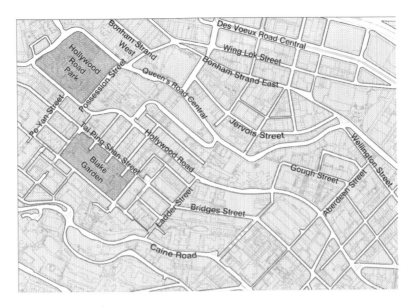

Map of Sheung Wan

The First Opium War ended with imperial China's humiliating defeat and the ceding of Hong Kong to Britain. In 1841, the British fleet docked at the west end of the newly minted crown colony and christened it "Victoria City." They set up barracks on Possession Street where the present day Hollywood Road Park is located. Newcomers from Europe soon fanned out along the northwestern coastline and up the north slope of Victoria Peak. The Chinese called these settlements the "Four Rings" (四環).

Sheung Wan, which means the "upper ring" in Cantonese, was flanked on the west by Sai Wan (the west ring) and on the east by Central (the middle ring). The local population at the time numbered only a few thousand. They comprised mainly farmers, fishermen, incense makers and manual laborers referred to as "coolies." Life went on for the most part, as the foreigners gradually transformed the barren island into a modern European city.

The new colony was a tough place on a good day – the heat, the humidity and the constant threat of pirates. However, it was the native population that proved to be the real nuisance. In the eyes of the ruling elite, the Chinese were uncivilized and unfit to live among them. Not long after the British settled in, the locals were summarily removed from Central – the *de facto* capital of Hong Kong – and shoved into Sheung Wan. A self-sustaining shantytown began to coagulate on Tai Ping Shan Street, resulting in a dense terrain of tenement houses covering an area the size of a few soccer fields. Aberdeen Street was the border separating the white community from the yellow ghetto.

When life gave the Chinese a lemon, they didn't just make lemonade. They also built a sidewalk stand and turned it into a global enterprise. The dense population on Tai Ping Shan Street provided the cheap labor needed to develop Sheung Wan into the busiest trading port in the Far East. Bonham Strand became today's equivalent of a container terminal, where cargo ships would dock and coolies would load and unload containers like an army of ants. When the northerly winds blew, merchant ships would sail downwind to mainland China loading up on rice, cooking oil, spices and beans. When the gale turned southerly, the goods would be distributed all over South East Asia and sold at a premium. Companies engaged in this latitudinal import-export business were dubbed "North and South Houses" (南北行). They numbered around 300 by the turn of the 20th Century, a few of which are still in business on Bonham Strand today.

As the trading business thrived, auxiliary services began to emerge. Man Mo Temple (文武廟) on Hollywood Road doubled as a town hall where commercial disputes were arbitrated outside the colonial courts. By the 1880s, the first Chinese banks opened on Wing Lok Street. One of them was a small foreign exchange shop that went by the name Hang Seng. This humble Sheung Wan outfit would become the second largest retail bank in Hong Kong. Asia's best known stock index would be named after it.

Man Mo Temple on Hollywood Road was built in 1847

Over just one generation, the Sheung Wan population exploded from 5,000 in 1841 to 150,000 in 1871. The growth was triggered in part by increased employment and in part by the massive influx of mainland Chinese escaping from the Taiping Rebellion (太平天國). As the population density rose, so did its vulnerability to natural disasters. The Great Fire of 1851, for instance, destroyed hundreds of tenement houses and led to the reconstruction of a large portion of Sheung Wan. Bonham Strand and Jervois Street were named after the governor and his deputy who oversaw the project. The area was decimated again two decades later, when the Typhoon of 1874 leveled coastal settlements. The storm claimed

2,000 lives and made international headlines. According to one eyewitness, corpses were strewn all along the harbor and had to be hastily buried for fear of an outbreak of disease.

Sanitation among the Chinese population was the biggest headache for the British. Living conditions were particularly deplorable on overcrowded Tai Ping Shan Street. Many of its residents remained agrarian, living side-by-side with hogs, fowls and other farm animals. Modern plumbing and clean water supplies were rare. To the Europeans living next door in Central and Midlevels, it was a problem that even geographical segregation could not solve. When it comes to pests and disease, out-of-sight is hardly out-of-mind.

Concerted efforts by both British authorities and local community leaders were made to improve hygiene and healthcare. In 1870, the colonial government financed the construction of Tung Wah Hospital (東華醫院) on Po Yan Street. It was the colony's first dispensary of traditional Chinese medical care. In 1887, local philanthropist Dr. Ho Kai (何啟) founded the Hong Kong College of Medicine for Chinese at the intersection of Hollywood Road and Aberdeen Street. It was the first of its kind to train Cantonese speaking doctors in Western medicine. The college would be the forerunner of the University of Hong Kong. Dr. Sun Yat-sen, its famous alumnus, would alter the course of history by plotting a nationwide revolution against imperial China with his classmates on Gough Street. Dr. Sun would go on to become the founding father of the new Republic of China.

No amount of hospitals or doctors, however revolutionary, would prepare the colony for the horror of what was to come. In 1894, the bubonic plague arrived in the city from nearby Canton province. The disease, which was spread by rat-borne fleas, had a frightening mortality rate of 95%. Fearing a repeat of the Black

Death in medieval Europe, the British government moved swiftly and declared Hong Kong an infected port. An aggressive program was implemented to clean up Sheung Wan. British soldiers were mobilized to fumigate Chinese houses and round up the infected. Because half of all cases came from the Tai Ping Shan area, the British repossessed the 10 acres of land, demolished every house on it and rebuilt the area as a public park called Blake Garden (卜公花園), named after a former governor of Hong Kong.

As expected, draconian plague fighting measures were met with distrust and resistance from the local population. Isolation of patients aboard the hospital ship *Hygeia* raised the specter of organ harvesting. Chinese families were known to hide the sick and even dead bodies in their homes to evade forced removal and mass burial. The plague and ensuing events triggered a reverse exodus of local citizens back to Canton. A third of the Chinese population would seek refuge from their mainland relatives, rendering Sheung Wan a virtual ghost town.

With the colony's economy decimated by the pestilence, the British government committed to more than just disinfection and quarantine. In 1906, a bacteriological facility – the present day Museum of Medical Sciences – was built next to Blake Garden. International experts from England, France and Japan were brought in to treat the infected and develop a vaccine. Even so, outbreaks would return in fits and starts for another 30 years. By the time the bubonic plague was finally brought under control in 1925, the death toll in Hong Kong would top 20,000, 70 times the number lost to SARS in 2003.

Over the remainder of the century, Victoria City would evolve into the megalopolis we know today. Sheung Wan would be transformed into an eclectic milieu of posh restaurants, up-market galleries and swanky serviced apartments. It is now a *place de choix* for European expatriates lured by its unique blend of historical character and modern convenience. Even the once squalid Tai Ping Shan area has become a coveted residential enclave sought out by artists and epicureans. Ever resilient, the Upper Ring has risen from its checkered history of racial segregation and calamity, and has reinvented itself yet again.

* * *

Up the hill-hugging stairs of Ladder Street, a hundred yards above the *hoi polloi* cluttering Queen's Road, a pair of century-old banyans rise out of a granite wall. Mossy branches stretch far, aerial roots sway. Weathered trunks lean with avuncular benevolence. Amidst the thick tangle of alleys and lanes, every tree has a story to tell, each stone reveals a tale. Together they bear witness to a community woven of courage and grit, by the wheel of history that spares neither sweat nor blood. Sheung Wan is a living tree, its future ever evolving and its past a testament to the sacrifices of those who came before us. So there we have it, 170 years of history in a single neighborhood, a mere five-minute walk from the humdrum of Central.

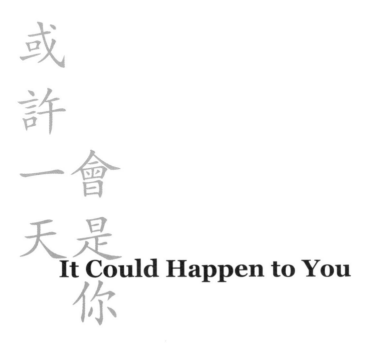

It Could Happen to You

Last Tuesday I had dinner with a few friends at a restaurant in Kennedy Town. At precisely 9:30pm, the entire restaurant, patrons and staff alike, came to an abrupt standstill. Children were hushed, the clinking of bowls and plates stopped. Everyone turned their heads to the flat screen television hung high from the ceiling. One of the waiters clicked the remote control to ATV, an unpopular local channel that almost nobody watches. It was the live broadcast of the Mark Six draw, a three times a week event that almost everybody watches.

By the time the plastic drum stopped turning and the seven golf balls lined up neatly on the bottom of the screen, the show was over. Patrons returned to their food and staff continued making beelines to and from the kitchen. Balled up tickets festooned the floor. But all was not lost: the estimated jackpot for Thursday's draw, just two days later, was expected to exceed HK$130 million (US$17 million), the biggest in the city's history.

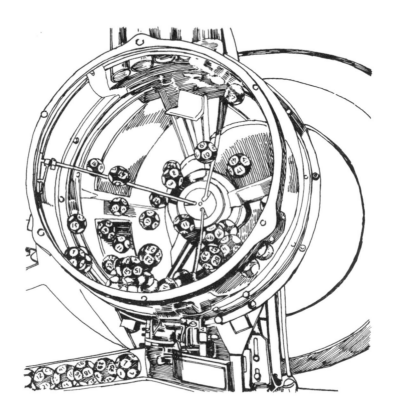

Hong Kong's most famous drum

Mark Six is the only legal form of lottery in Hong Kong. Nearly four decades since its introduction by the colonial government to combat underground gambling, the lottery remains the most popular game of chance in the city and the fastest way to rewrite a person's destiny. If we ever need to find a shibboleth to tell locals and foreigners apart, then the lottery's famous theme song, adopted from a 1972 hit by Dutch band Shocking Blue, would be it. If you can hum it from start to finish, then you are one of us.

When I was little, my father would decide what numbers to play by having my brother and me draw from a bag of marbles with numbers he had meticulously taped on each of them. According to Chinese folklore, young boys possess extraordinary luck in all forms of gambling. Despite not having any supernatural powers, I gladly answered my father's call — for who wouldn't want to be the boy angel who lifted his family from rags to riches?

The nine-digit prize money this Thursday had become the talk of the town. Even though the odds of winning were less than one in 140,000,000, I decided to join in the fun. On Wednesday afternoon, I visited one of the Jockey Club's betting branches, my first time ever. At the Stanley Street branch in Central, a queue of roughly 200 people hugged the block. I later learned that that particular branch was rumored to be the luckiest betting outpost in the city, where several first prize tickets had been sold in the past. Lucky or not, I wasn't about to spend an hour waiting in line and so I made my way to the Connaught Road location where the queue was noticeably shorter.

Inside the betting hall, I was surrounded by swarms of men and women of all ages. Some were lining up in front of the half dozen manned counters, while others were busily punching numbers at the umpteen self-service betting machines. It was a controlled chaos where the illusion of hope collided with an assault on the senses. The line at counter number four — a decidedly unpopular counter for its inauspiciousness — was moving quickly and in less than five minutes I walked out of the branch with a ticket in hand and high hopes in my head.

Lotteries are a near universal phenomenon, simultaneously a powerful agent of income redistribution and a ready means for governments to finance anything from wars to education. Prize money in the United States, especially the multi-state lotteries such as Powerball and Mega Millions, can reach billions of Hong Kong dollars. Even in nearby Taiwan, lottery jackpots are much larger than ours. In 2013, for instance, a lucky winner of the Super Lotto (威力彩) took home NT\$2.4 billion (HK\$630 million or US\$80 million) in cash, nearly five times this Thursday's record breaking jackpot. It seems a bit odd that, for a city known in the region for its vibrant horse racing scenes, Hong Kong should have so much catching up to do when it comes to the size of our lottery jackpot.

As is the case for many things in life, anticipation is often the best part of the experience. Thinking up ways to spend a sudden windfall is a form of entertainment in itself, enough to make a Jewish milkman break into song in *Fiddler on the Roof*. I too was forced to confront the very question of "if I were a rich man" when I was accosted by a young girl carrying a clipboard outside the betting station. She asked if I wanted to participate in a quick survey for an organization of which I had never heard. Even though I knew it was just a telemarketing trick to solicit personal details, I said "yes" just to see what questions she would ask. Sure enough, the selection of answers to her last question offered a glimpse of our collective psyche.

Question 5: What would you do with your prize money? (Circle all that apply)
  (A) purchase property
  (B) invest in the stock market
  (C) set up an education fund for your children
  (D) other uses

I couldn't think of more boring ways of spending my fortune and so I asked the girl to circle "D". Then it struck me that to many people in Hong Kong, the best way to spend one's money is simply to make more of it. Sad, but sublimely pragmatic. In the end the surveyor did not bother to find out what "other uses" I had in mind; and I never gave her the phone number that she so insistently demanded.

History has shown us time and again that winning a multi-million dollar jackpot can be more of a curse than a blessing. As a wise man once said: The thing about things you don't have, is that getting them is the last thing you need. In the U.S., for instance, lotteries reserve the right to publish the winners' names and places of work. As a result, winners of mega jackpots may suddenly be thrust into the intense media spotlight and find themselves in the unenviable position of having their way of life drastically and irreversibly altered.

One of the best examples of lottery-win-turned-nightmare was Jack Whittaker, the West Virginia businessman who won a US$315 million (HK$2.5 billion) Powerball lottery in 2007. In the years that followed, Whittaker's home and car were burglarized repeatedly, his employees embezzled company funds 11 times and 460 lawsuits were filed against him. In his darkest moments, his wife left him, his daughter was diagnosed with cancer and his granddaughter died from a drug overdose. "If it would bring back my old life, I'd give all the money back," Whittaker told a reporter.

Needless to say, I didn't win this Friday's lottery. Instead, the HK$130 million jackpot went to three winners whose destinies were about to be rewritten, for better or for worse. If I had won, I know I would never spend another day in the office and would split my time between a summer villa in Tuscany and a three-story mansion on the Peak, all the while buying things I never thought I would need – a Lamborghini, a golf club membership and one of those diamond studded Vertu cell phones. Since I didn't win, I have been spared the trials of Jack Whittaker and many others who have won billions but lost so much more. I consider that a well hedged bet.

Hong Kong Hold'em

The taxi got off the main road and pulled up at a *cul-de-sac* in the upscale neighborhood of Happy Valley. The sidewalk was deserted and drenched in streetlights. A stray dog barked in the distance. I tiptoed up the stairs to the third floor of a post-war tenement building and checked the number on the door. Unit 3B. I knocked twice, and a middle-aged Australian man named James answered the door.

"Is this where the game is?" I asked with mock confidence. The host nodded and ushered me into the apartment.

In the dining room, four other men slouched at an oval table. They sized me up before offering me a seat next to an Irishman named Howard. The rotund redhead took a sip of beer and began shuffling cards with the dexterity of a Vegas croupier, reeking of testosterone.

It was Poker Wednesday at the Harrison's.

A home game at the Harrisons

On any given night, home games are hosted across Hong Kong. Poker is a popular pastime in the expat community and Texas hold'em is the game of choice. Each player makes the best five-card hand by combining two private cards with three out of the five public cards placed face up in the middle of the table. I learned the rules from watching the annual World Series of Poker on ESPN.

On amateur nights like this one, there is no fancy green felt or dark sunglasses to hide poker tells. All you need is two cheap decks of cards from 7-Eleven, a set of chips and a stomach for free-flowing beer and trash talk. By the end of the night, the winner pays for pizza, and the loser goes home with a broken piggybank and a bruised ego.

I swear I went to the Harrison's for research only. That's what gamblers tell their wives. Whatever my motivation was, I was certain to meet a menagerie of characters. There were five of them: the Screamer, the Sweater, the Rookie, his mentor Howard, and the host James Harrison, a.k.a. the Folder because he would fold every time he wasn't dealt face cards. They were all Caucasians in their 40s, law firm partners who got together once a week to have a boys' night in.

Then there was me, the lone Chinese guy who stepped in as a last minute substitute for a regular who had called in sick. I knew enough to play but I still struggled to keep up with the game's dizzying jargon. In Texas hold'em, a player must call, check, raise or fold, and the dealer must burn and turn. There are the flops and the river, the big blind, the small blind, and the double blind.

The penalty for mistakes can be hefty. The minimum buy-in at tonight's game was HK$3,000 (US$385), which is modest compared to some of the serious games that can run up to several hundred thousand dollars. Within the expat community, there is no shortage of high-rollers who are in it for more than weeknight entertainment with the boys.

Gambling takes on many forms in Hong Kong: the lottery, horse races and betting on soccer games. Gambling is legal only if it is run by the Jockey Club, which has a monopoly on all gaming activities. A notable exception is mahjong, that beloved social pastime for Chinese people around the world. Under Hong Kong law, mahjong can be played at licensed gaming parlors, at restaurants or at home. Poker, on the other hand, has yet to catch on with the local population. Its legality remains ambiguous.

Until 2010, a handful of commercial poker houses operated openly in Central and Causeway Bay, drawing hundreds of mostly expat players every night. To comply with gambling laws, they operated as private clubs where members played against each other on "social occasions" and the operators took no profit from the games. For all intents and purposes, poker houses were no different from the bridge room at a country club or the cluster of mahjong tables at a Chinese wedding banquet.

A high profile police raid in the summer of 2010 put an end to the at-large poker scene. On a sweltering August night, law enforcement swamped the Hong Kong Poker House on Hollywood Road and arrested everyone on the premises, despite vehement protest from the poker house that no law had been broken. Angry players, a majority of them lawyers, bankers and hedge fund managers with big egos and little patience, spent a sleepless night at the Sheung Wan police precinct and ended up on the front page of the *Apple Daily* looking like hardened criminals. In the end no charges were pressed, but the damage was done. Other poker houses in the city began to vanish and citizens became gun-shy about playing cards in public places. Those who want to get their fix, however, can still do so in the privacy of their own homes or hop on a ferry to Macau.

The police crackdown on recreational poker sparked an outrage in the expat community. As unjust and unjustified as the poker bust was to some people, it didn't surprise those of us who understand how our city is governed. Indeed, the raid was entirely consistent with the police's "one size fits all" approach to issues they don't understand.

Drugs are a good example. In the eyes of the police, drugs are just that: drugs. Never mind the distinction between soft drugs like marijuana and hard drugs like cocaine and heroin, users of all banned substances are arrested and prosecuted with equal fervor.

Likewise for gambling, law enforcement considers any activity outside the purview of the do-no-evil Jockey Club a threat to society. In their minds, the idea of a poker house conjures up images of a seedy gambling ring run by tattooed triad members who prey on vulnerable citizens and turn our wholesome city into a modern day Sodom and Gomorrah.

The truth is, hold'em is a highly social form of entertainment just like mahjong, chess or karaoke. It is fun and it requires skill. But don't tell that to the police. With the way things are going, it will be years before Hong Kongers feel comfortable playing poker in bars, restaurants or other public places without fear of police reprisals.

If the Harrison's hideout represented the underworld of the expat gambling scene in Hong Kong, then I was in for a big disappointment. Tattooed gangsters were nowhere in sight. Nor were there loan sharks lurking about in dark corners. At 11:30pm, Mrs. Harrison came home from the movies and poked her head into the dining room.

"How was the game, hon?" Her question doubled as a cue for us to call it a night. The Folder heaved a sigh and said, "I've played better." That night he lost a half month's rent. The Irishman, on the other hand, netted nearly ten grand and paid for pizza.

As for myself, like I said, I was only there for the research.

可
笑
的
情
人

My Funny Valentine

Valentine's Day is, for many, the most dreaded holiday on the calendar. Those who are already spoken for go along with it and pretend to enjoy it. For 24 hours, they act as though their love were as sweet as Godiva chocolates and their lives as rosy as an Agnes B flower bouquet. Singles, on the other hand, are relegated to spending the night alone at home with a tub of Häagen-Dazs in front of the television or meeting up with other singles to commiserate the way the years have slipped through their fingers. No one wants to be a wall flower or shrinking violet.

Valentine's Day is a quintessential Hallmark holiday. It was conceived, created and blown out of proportion by florists and chocolate makers. Originally dedicated to the Valentine of Rome, a martyred priest in the Middle Ages, the holiday was later removed from the Christian calendar because there wasn't much to celebrate. Historically, the day had nothing to do with either love or romance, until English poet Geoffrey Chaucer associated the fateful day with a pair of love birds in an obscure 15th Century poem. Chaucer could never have imagined the magnitude of harm he would inflict on mankind, nor could he have guessed that his words would lead to cash registers around the world ringing non-stop on the horrid winter day.

Different cultures celebrate Valentine's Day in their own unique way. While the Western world sticks to the chauvinistic tradition of men buying women trinkets, most Arab countries ban Valentine's Day merchandise as they are considered too Christian for comfort. In Japan and Korea, the gift giving customs are reversed. Women are obligated to give chocolates to not only their other halves but also every male coworker in the office. A month later on March 14, dubbed the "White Day," the tables are turned and men reciprocate with bigger gifts. Valentine's Day is such a huge industry in Japan that February 14 accounts for half of the country's annual chocolate sales.

In Hong Kong where everything is measured in dollars and cents, lovers take Valentine's Day celebrations to a whole new level. The clock has barely struck 9am when the first flower delivery arrives in the office at the third cubicle in the first row – two dozen long stem roses from Jacqueline's doting husband, one for each year of marriage. Then one delivery after another, expensive bouquets go to Mary, Susie, Cindy and Queenie, each one bigger and more impressive than the last. The intra-office popularity contest continues throughout the morning. The winner, crowned the Mrs. with the Mostest, will get a day of bragging rights in the department. The losers – ladies who haven't received anything by lunch time – will keep their heads down for the rest of the day and make excuses for their negligent husbands or imaginary boyfriends. That explains why a large number of men are said to be "on a business trip" every 14 February.

I love you enough to overpay for these

Another funny – and expensive – aspect of Valentine's Day in Hong Kong is dining out. Restaurants are booked solid weeks in advance. Seating by the window must be reserved three months ahead of time. If a miracle happens and you manage to find a table, you are handed the special Valentine's set dinner menu designed to trap silly couples who are too smitten to notice the steep prices. Who could have guessed that mushroom soup with rose petals and heart-shaped sirloin on February 14 would cost five times more than mushroom soup without rose petals and regularly-shaped sirloin just the day before? Here is a piece of advice: if you must celebrate this silly holiday, then do your wallet a favor and eat out the week before.

Valentine's Day is as contrived as it is an unnecessary source of stress for everyone, single or otherwise. Until we realize that gift giving is only sweet when it is unexpected, all those obligatory flowers and chocolates are wasted in exchange for a fleeting moment of self-validation. Nevertheless, Valentine's Day does serve as an important reminder that relationships are based on unconditional sacrifices and mutual gratification no matter the cost. If you look at it that way, maybe the holiday does have some meaning after all.

不看書的城市

The City that Doesn't Read

The Hong Kong Book Fair is the city's biggest literary event, drawing millions of visitors every July.

The operative word in the preceding sentence is "visitors," for many of them aren't exactly readers. A good number show up to *tsau yit lau* (湊熱鬧), or literally, to go where the noise is. In recent years, the week-long event has taken on a theme park atmosphere. It is where bargain hunters fill up empty suitcases with discounted books, where young entrepreneurs wait all night for autographed copies only to resell them on eBay, and where barely legal – and barely dressed – teenage models promote their latest photo albums. And why not? Hong Kongers love a carnival. How many people visit a Chinese New Year flower market to actually buy flowers?

If books are nourishment for the soul, then the soul of our city must have gone on a diet. In Hong Kong, not enough of us read and we don't read enough. That makes us an "aliterate" people: able to read but not interested in reading. According to a study by Lingnan University, 42% of the local population does not read anything other than magazines and newspapers. The actual percentage is likely higher, considering that some respondents may feel embarrassed to admit they don't read, while others may have counted flipping through a travel guide or looking up a word in the dictionary as reading. If you think I'm being cynical, ask 10 people you know and see how many of them can name the author of *Dream of the Red Chamber* (《紅樓夢》), one of the four great classics in the Chinese canon. How many of them actually think Franz Kafka is a luxury watch brand?

So what went wrong?

The intuitive answer is stress. Life in Hong Kong sometimes feels like an never-ending daisy chain of deadlines and to-do lists, and the last thing we want to do after a 14-hour work day is to pick up an epic novel printed in eight point font. A common complaint I hear from my friends is that reading tires their eyes and puts them to sleep.

But the stress argument doesn't pass muster. First of all, books are just like movies – they are a form of escapist entertainment. If *Patton* or *Schindler's List* is too heavy, then go with a comedy or an anime. You don't have to choose Shakespeare or Kierkegaard for bedtime reading. Second, we are hardly the only people under stress. The Japanese and the Koreans, for instance, have equally demanding lives and face an even more oppressive office culture. Subway trains in Tokyo and Seoul are packed with commuters whose noses are buried in paperback novels. By contrast, in Hong Kong we rarely find readers on any mode of public transport. It is always easy to pick out Hong Kong vacationers in beach resorts like Bali and Phuket – they are the only people carrying a tabloid magazine instead of a book.

If stress doesn't explain our bibliophobia, then there must be something about our culture. Reading, like brushing our teeth and eating vegetables, starts from an early age. The habit begins at home. Whereas it is common in the West for families to have a small library at home, very few families in Hong Kong see the need – or have the space – to do so. According to the same Lingnan University study, 14% of local homes do not have a single book other than textbooks. To many young children, reading for pleasure is considered a distraction from school work. Worse still, children who read books can be branded as antisocial and, in the age of the iPad and Xbox, rather uncool. The situation doesn't get better with age, as constant internal assessments at school bear down on students and the threat of make-or-break public exams loom large. As a result, local students applying for university are invariably tripped up by one simple question on the application form: *What was your favorite book read outside class in the past twelve months and why?*

Out in the real world, reading seems even more irrelevant. Hong Kongers pride themselves on being fast thinkers and smart workers. We put in minimum effort and get maximum results. Who needs books when we have Wikipedia and Google? As more and more citizens get their news from online sources, even tabloid magazines and free newspapers – the literary staple of

42% of the population – are facing obsolescence. The cultural desert is getting dryer by the day.

While nearly half of Hong Kongers don't read, everyone seems to appreciate the benefits of reading. Every weekend, bookstores across the city are packed with parents binge shopping for their kids, from pop-up books to world classics and biographies of scions and celebrities. When it comes to nourishing young minds, money is no object. In fact, children's books now account for nearly half of book sales in Hong Kong. The rationale is simple: children need to appear well read to get into good schools. But that's hardly the way to foster a reading environment at home. If mom and dad themselves do not read, then reading is simply one of those things that children are forced to do, like playing the violin or practicing karate. Very few end up keeping up with their childhood hobbies as they grow up.

Some children read, but most adults don't

Turning to the 58% of the population that claims to be regular readers, the question becomes *what* they read. A survey by a local think tank indicates that less than half of the respondents are interested in fiction. The majority of readers go for the usual suspects: finance, self-help, travel, health and astrology. There are very few local novelists in Hong Kong, and the only fiction genres that sell well are martial arts and Danielle Steel-esque romance. Let's face it, Hong Kong is a utilitarian society. Everything we do must serve a purpose and the purpose is usually rooted in money. Non-fiction is popular because it is considered more "useful." Fiction, on the other hand, is often dismissed as a waste of time or a luxury for retirees. Never mind that research after research has shown that reading even short stories can improve our cognitive abilities and help us exercise better judgment.

I grew up in a family of readers. My father worked in the newspaper industry, which helped instill in all of us an appreciation for the written word. There were books all around the house and we could always pick one up and start reading. We did it not because it would make us smarter or more knowledgeable, but because the books were just there. Once we started the first chapter, we wouldn't be able to put it down. This was especially true with fiction, which took us to different places and different times. My parents never had to force us to read – it just happened naturally.

If there is one thing I learned from my childhood, it is that access holds the key to cultivating a reading habit. Perhaps that's what the Hong Kong Book Fair hopes to achieve: to increase access to books for millions of aliterate citizens. Anything that brings people closer to the printed word, even only for a week, cannot be a bad thing. So bring on the teenage models.

燒
烤
文
化

Cookout Culture

Everyone loves a barbecue. The primal way of cooking food on an open fire transcends time and culture. The Koreans, the Mongolians and folks from the Middle East are well known lovers of grilled meat. Nevertheless, it is the Americans who have elevated it to a national pastime. In Anytown, USA, no suburban home is complete without a propane grill in the backyard, ready to be deployed on a sunny weekend.

A "cookout" – as outdoor barbecuing is affectionately termed in America – is more than just a meal. It is a wholesome gathering that brings together friends and family. It is also an important bonding ritual that lasts all afternoon and empties cases of beer. If the purpose of a dinner party is to showcase the host's good taste and attention to detail, then a barbecue is meant to play up his fun-loving, spontaneous side.

Hong Kongers love anything barbecued. *Siu mei* (燒味), or roast meat, is a staple on any Cantonese menu. In Hong Kong, a Chinese chef's culinary skills are often judged by the simple task of preparing good barbecued pork or *char siu* (叉燒). Made with pork shoulder and seasoned with honey and dark soy sauce, *char siu* can make or break a restaurant. *Char siu fan* (叉燒飯), or barbecued pork over rice, is such a common dish for the masses that it is used as a measure of inflation. Older folks like to lament how *char siu fan* used to cost less than HK$10 (US$1.30), before they lecture us on the virtue of saving.

Our love for grilling is not limited to the indoors. We love a good cookout as much as the Americans, if not more. While people on the other side of the Pacific will only have a barbecue during the warmer months between April and November, Hong Kongers do it all year long. Another key difference between our cookout and theirs is the equipment. Because very few people in Hong Kong have a backyard and using a propane grill on a balcony is against the fire code, everyone goes to public barbecue pits. Located on the beach or in large rural parks, these pits are simple square-shaped stone troughs to be filled with wood charcoal. Food items are then skewered on two-prong spits and placed over the open fire. The spit looks like a tuning fork used in piano class with the length of a tennis racket.

Still another difference between a Hong Kong style cookout and the American version is the choice of food. In the U.S., barbecue must haves include hamburgers, hotdogs and spare ribs. The fancier host will prepare vegetable skewers with bell peppers, mushrooms and zucchini. Children will insist on grilling marshmallows to make s'mores. In Hong Kong, BBQs are a meat lover's heaven and a vegetarian's hell. The menu is almost exclusively carnivorous, with an occasional sweet potato or corn on the cob tossed in if you are lucky. There are chicken wings, hot dog sausages, beef steaks, pork chops, lamb chops and meatballs of every kind. Meats are purchased pre-marinated either from a supermarket or the mom-and-pop convenience store near the barbecue site. No matter how much food you buy, it will never break the piggy bank. You can easily feed a hungry group of 12 for under HK$500 (US$80), which makes BBQ an affordable form of weekend entertainment.

A national pastime in Hong Kong

A Hong Kong style BBQ is not only cheap, it also teaches us important life skills. It is the closest we come to experiencing wilderness survival. Before we start grilling, we must first make a fire. The inexperienced can struggle all night trying to get the fire going, while strangers look on with pity. Once the charcoal is lit, however, it is all fun and games. Like fishing and playing mahjong, barbecue lends itself to great conversations. Some of the best heart-to-heart talks and gossip sessions happen around the campfire.

Each time I propose a Hong Kong style BBQ, I hear grumblings from my expat friends. While they like the idea of eating outdoors (as all foreigners do), the more finicky ones are put off by the all meat menu and the fact that everyone has to get their hands dirty. As the night falls and the conversations start to pick up, however, even the biggest skeptic will warm to the idea and start jabbing that tuning fork into a hunk of meat.

Other than skeptics, I also have to deal with the novice in every group. There are three pieces of advice I offer these barbecue virgins.

First, *keep your eye on the food*. It only takes a few minutes for the meat to get burned. It is a pitfall for untrained grillers who are easily distracted by the fireside chat. These incidents never go unnoticed and they will always elicit the same response from the locals: "Don't eat it, charred food gives you cancer!" To avoid premature death, you are well advised to mimic an oven rotisserie and rotate the spit at a controlled speed of roughly three revolutions per minute. When the meat is almost done, glaze it generously with honey which will bring out the savory taste of the grilled meat.

Second, *cook your own food*. A Hong Kong style BBQ is like a reality show: every man fends for himself. Given all the hard work that goes into skewering, grilling and glazing the meat, it is bad form to ask for food and it is equally inappropriate to offer it, because it will invariably make the rest of the people look bad and feel obligated to do the same. We as a society have decided to follow the 11th Commandment of "thou shalt not covet thy neighbor's chicken wings."

Third, *eat turtle shell jelly the following day*. Yes, I said turtle shell jelly. Every Hong Konger subscribes to the folk belief that grilled meat is the king of "fiery foods" which causes the *yang* (陽) in your body to overpower the *yin* (陰). The resulting ailment is called *yit hey* (熱氣; literally, hot energy). The symptoms include bad skin, sore throats and oral ulcers. The best way to restore the inner balance is by eating turtle shell jelly available at fine herbal shops everywhere. I am a strong believer in the gelatinous remedy, although I concede that it is a bit of an acquired taste.

Because wood charcoal is an indispensable part of a Hong Kong style barbecue, its storied past is worth a mention. Charcoal is an impure form of carbon made by heating wood in the absence of oxygen. When it burns, it releases a trace amount of carbon monoxide, a colorless, odorless and highly toxic gas. When used outdoors at the barbecue pit, charcoal is perfectly safe as the carbon monoxide will dissipate into the air. Used indoors without proper ventilation, however, it can release enough toxic gas to kill a person in less than an hour. During the 1997-98 Asian Financial Crisis, "charcoal burning" became the suicide method of choice among people who lost their homes to foreclosure. They would check into a rental apartment in Cheung Chau or Shek O (both popular barbecue sites where carrying a bag of charcoal would not arouse suspicion), close the windows and lock themselves in, before setting a fire that would begin a slow, painless death. Compared to jumping off a bridge or slitting one's wrist, carbon monoxide poisoning seems like a good way to go.

Barbecues are a quintessential Hong Kong pastime – it is an activity everyone grows up doing. To make the experience even more foolproof, storeowners near popular BBQ sites have in recent years begun renting out private pits to partygoers. Private pits are popular because they are in a covered area and the pit owner supplies both the food and equipment. He will even make the fire for you. Convenient though it may be, the idea does not appeal to barbecue purists such as myself. After all, shopping for my own food and starting my own fire are all part and parcel of the authentic cookout experience. If we don't hold the line on our tradition, next thing you know our food will be grilled *for* us in an air-conditioned room. Then we might as well just have Korean barbecue.

*   *   *

A checklist for a Hong Kong style barbecue:

- pre-marinated meats of every kind
- sweet potatoes
- corn on the cob
- honey (with brush)
- spit (one per person, plus an extra one to spread the charcoal)
- wood charcoal (two large bags)
- fire starters (one box)
- lighter
- steel gauze
- aluminum foil (to wrap the vegetables)
- worker's gloves (to handle the charcoal)
- plastic plates and forks
- paper napkins
- old newspapers (to fan the fire)

No Place Like Home

Canto pop singer/songwriter Sam Hui is a cultural icon. He used catchy tunes and biting lyrics to chronicle the city's social history in the 1970s and 80s, a period often associated with blue collar jobs, rising food prices and water rationing. Hui is also an ardent Hongkongophile. In one of his best known hits, *Cloud-reaching Tower* (《鐵塔凌雲》), he compares the city to the world's great sights. The Eiffel Tower and the Statue of Liberty, he laments, don't tug at his heartstrings. Mount Fuji and Hawaiian beaches, with all their grandeur, pale in comparison to the tiny boat lights that dot the harbor at home.

I have lived in Hong Kong long enough to feel the same gravitational pull that Hui sings about. Every time I travel overseas – about two dozen times a year – I am reminded of how attached I am to the city. I could be relaxing on a Balinese beach or sauntering down the tree-lined Champs Élysées in Paris and my mind will suddenly drift back to the maddening island. I may wonder what is on the evening news and what my friends are saying about it. Is my mailbox full? Has it been raining much? I may get a little homesick.

What is it about this place that makes us miss it on Day 3 of our vacation? What *je ne sais quoi* does it possess that makes relocating to Shanghai or Sydney feel like a death sentence? Yes, we have the world's most amazing skyline and no, we don't have any sales tax. We have a great infrastructure and our healthcare system is not bad either. But that is *not* it. When we are lying in the hotel bed staring at the ceiling, we think only of the little things. True love, after all, is *always* about the little things.

I decided to grab a notepad and scribble a list of small miracles in the city that have made our lives infinitely better. They are what magazine columnists like to call the "10 things I can't live without." The items may seem random but, then again, so may the reasons why you married your spouse.

1. Octopus card – This Hong Kong invention has made cashless payment a reality. It is believed to have inspired London's Oyster Card and Japan's Suica. The technology is now going to mainland China, New Zealand, the Netherlands and the Middle East. In Hong Kong, the Octopus has extended its tentacles everywhere from public transport to convenience stores, coffee shops, car parks, fast food chains and, *apropos*, swimming pools. We can't and won't leave home without it. There are some things money can't buy, for everything else there's... *DOOD!*

The card that makes the famous "dood" sound

2. Central escalators – Whoever came up with the idea of lining our steep terrain with outdoor escalators must have been ridiculed at first. Guess who's laughing now? The conveyance system connecting Queen's Road to Conduit Road has done wonders for the area by drastically improving its connectivity and bringing life to neighborhoods like SoHo and NoHo. It has been such a smashing success that the concept is being replicated in hilly areas across the island. That's right, us hipsters don't bother with taxis or trains – we take the escalators home.

3. Curry fish balls – We don't know if they are actually made from fish, but who gives a rat? We love street food and we love street food on skewers even more. Like stinky tofu and stuffed bell peppers, curry fish balls are cheap and delicious. I call them "dim sum for the masses." Concerns about hygiene and public safety, however, have moved food vendors off the streets into brick and mortar shops. Don't let the modest storefront fool you. Popular joints in Causeway Bay and Mongkok have made millionaires out of fish ballers.

4. Beef chow fun – It is the ultimate comfort food for the Cantonese people, the cultural equivalent of a cheeseburger in America or fish and chips in England. The chef tosses the simple ingredients of beef, rice noodles and bean sprouts in a giant wok and stir fries them over an industrial strength burner. The result is so *mmm mmm* good that we are willing to overlook the copious amounts of grease and salt. If I ever find myself on death row, consider this my last meal request.

5. Iced tea in a box – Anywhere else in the world, boxed drinks are only for children. Here in Hong Kong, they are consumed by people of all ages. Grown men in pinstripe suits and fashionistas in five-inch stilettos can be seen sucking on a little bendy straw inserted in a 2.5" by 4" box. Among the garden variety of boxed drinks available at 7-Eleven, the most popular is the lemon iced tea by Vitasoy, a leading local beverage maker. The drink is the perfect antidote to our summer heat in a delightfully squeezable package. The company came out with a bottled version years ago but it never caught on locally. No thanks, we say, the paper box will do just fine.

6. Outdoor drinking – Newcomers to Hong Kong from America, Canada, Australia and France are in for a pleasant surprise: they can booze in the great outdoors! Our lax drinking law might not be a big deal to us, but it is to people from countries where chugging a beer on a sidewalk or sipping champagne in a park can land them in jail. Hong Kong is a nanny state in many ways – smoking is prohibited everywhere, using profanity can get a teacher fired, and escalators keep screaming at us to "please hold the handrail." Not when it comes to regulating alcohol. We can all drink to that.

7. *Hiking trails* – For a concrete jungle, Hong Kong is surprisingly green. In fact, over two thirds of its land area is covered by thick vegetation, most of it is pristine rural parks. Cutting through the rolling mountains and plunging ravines are mile upon mile of perfectly groomed hiking trails, garnished with exotic plants and ribbons of waterfalls. The four major trails – MacLehose, Wilson, Hong Kong and Lantau – are our natural remedy for obesity, heart disease and depression. If it weren't for them, all we would do on the weekend is shop and eat.

8. *Victoria Park* – On the fringe of bustling Causeway Bay is 180,000 square feet of green space open to the public 24 hours a day. Vic Park is home to a half dozen concrete soccer fields (a novelty to foreigners), a generous open lawn (a novelty to locals) and a bronze statue of Queen Victoria (a novelty to mainland visitors). It is also the designated venue for celebrating Chinese New Year and the Mid-autumn Festival, as well as for housing political gatherings including the Tiananmen Square Massacre candlelight vigil every 4 June. The park is the lungs and the conscience of the city.

9. *Apliu Street* – Somewhere in dizzying Sham Shui Po is a paradise for tech geeks, handymen and frequent travelers. The Apliu Street (鴨寮街) flea market sells everything from LED flashlights to second hand loudspeakers and voltage converters. It is Radio Shack, Best Buy and Home Depot all rolled into one. Prices there are shockingly low. An electrical adaptor that sells for £19.95 at Heathrow Airport can be found here for HK$5 (US$0.65) apiece. And that's *before* you haggle.

10. Canto pop – I don't mean the karaoke kitsch beginning in the 1990s; I'm talking about the good stuff in the preceding two decades by the likes of Anita Mui, George Lam, Alan Tam and, of course, Sam Hui. These names may not mean much to an expat or anyone born in the new millennium, but their music is the soundtrack to my generation. Those mix tapes and homemade compilation CDs were what got me through boarding school and law school, offering a remedy to the homesickness and heartsickness that came with being far from home. They are the veritable chicken soup for the soul.

* * *

It is easy to be cynical about Hong Kong. The noise, the crowds and the stress put a permanent long face on the city. Every public holiday has become an excuse to get away, the farther the better. We pack a suitcase, fly three thousand miles to a beach resort and sign off from the urban ennui. But even the darkest of sunglasses cannot hide the fact that we are all Hongkongophiles deep inside. Not long after our second margarita, those little things – the "tiny boat lights" in Sam Hui's words – will creep back into our consciousness and tug gently at our hearts. The drips will turn into a trickle, and the trickle into a flood, until a smile finally lifts the corner of our mouths and we say to ourselves: There is no place like home.

Part 3
Our Identity

身份證

HKID

I lost my wallet a few weeks ago. As soon as I realized I had left it in a taxi, I called the dispatcher for help. I pleaded with the operator, only to be told bluntly that they didn't have a lost and found department.

Losing my wallet isn't such a big deal – I never carry much cash and credit cards can be easily replaced – except for my HKID, the photo identification that every citizen is required by law to carry at all times. In Hong Kong, police can stop anyone in his tracks and demand to see this document with or without probable cause. It is as if we need to constantly defend our status and assert our identity.

Next thing I knew, I was at the police headquarters in Admiralty making a statement. After that I rushed over to the Wanchai Government Tower, where I took a number and filled out some forms. I waited in line, paid a fee, had my photo taken, waited some more and sat down for an interview with an immigration officer. All that running around, plus the temporary loss of identity, had led to a mild existential crisis.

Our identity has always been a subject of contention. Most of us aren't even sure what to call ourselves. Ask anyone on the street that question and you will get a variety of answers: "Hong Konger," "Hong Kong Chinese," "Chinese Hong Konger" or, simply, "Chinese." These labels may sound the same to the untrained ear but not to us. With tensions between Hong Kong and the mainland growing by the day, we are increasingly mincing words and splitting hairs to distance ourselves from the Motherland. We draw a line in the sand and swear to defend our national identity – or something that resembles one.

In a recent survey conducted by the University of Hong Kong, the percentage of respondents who identified themselves distinctly as "Hong Kongers" – the only option without the word "Chinese" in it – hit an all-time high of 38%. That's twice as high as the percentage of respondents who identified themselves as "Chinese." The sentiment was most pronounced among our youth. A whopping 70% of respondents aged between 18 and 29 checked the "Hong Konger" box while less than 10% picked "Chinese." Indeed, "I'm not Chinese" is a declaration that echoes within Facebook walls and Golden Forum (高登), a popular chat room and a windsock of public opinion. Gone are the days when we sang about being "Descendants of the Dragon" and celebrated our black hair and yellow complexion with pride.

Our identity crisis is nothing new. For 150 years, Hong Kong was a foster child raised by a white family. Chinese born and British bred, the child ended up being neither. But he grew up all right – vibrant, prosperous and the envy of his Asian peers. The city was doing so well that it became an asylum for mainlanders escaping from war, famine and political turmoil. The influx of refugees surged between the 1950s and 70s, when China was ravaged by Mao Zedong's Shakespearean-in-magnitude power struggles. During those three decades, hundreds of thousands of defectors swam across Shenzhen Bay to the British colony and never looked back. Hong Kong was a city of Chinese who no longer wanted to be Chinese.

Our identity crisis deepened in the 1980s during the handover talks between Britain and China. The foster child was told that he would be going home to his biological parents, whether he liked it or not. But the generation gap between the two was too wide to bridge. Parent and child had close to nothing in common – they didn't even speak the same language, both literally and figuratively. To pacify its lost child, China offered the city a 50-year probation under the "one country, two systems" banner. "Nothing needs to change," the parent wooed, "and throw out that little red book if it scares you."

In the lead-up to the handover, no amount of cajoling by Communist China could stop nervous citizens from fleeing Hong Kong *en masse* to countries like Australia, Canada and the U.S. Horrendous images of the Tiananmen Square Massacre only accelerated the exodus. Kai Tak Airport in 1989 looked like Saigon in 1975. As a result of the Hong Kong Diaspora, a good number of citizens travel under multiple identities like covert CIA agents. We go in and out of countries using several different passports: Chinese, Canadian and that infamous "BNO" – the rather useless British National Overseas passport that confers neither a right of abode nor diplomatic protection. Each time we fill out a form, we have to pause for a few seconds and ponder what to put under "nationality."

The post-handover era saw the rise of the New China. The Motherland is now the world's second largest economy and a superpower with which the West must reckon. Instead of filling us with pride, China's ascent has turned us off even more. For every uplifting story of economic achievement and outer space breakthrough, there are hundreds more stomach turning scandals. People in Hong Kong are bombarded with a daily barrage of exposés about widespread corruption and business malpractice on the mainland. If it isn't a party princeling caught in a hit and run in daddy's Lamborghini, it's an industrial plant dumping carcinogens into a drinking water source. These days, "Made in China" means not only T-shirts and sneakers, but also fake phones, tainted baby formula and phony college degrees. All that, plus the country's tattered human rights records, feeds into the perception that the New China is a morally bankrupt Wild Wild East. We don't want to touch it with a ten-foot pole.

The more the wayward child retreats, the more the parent pursues. Since Hong Kong became a "special administrative region" in 1997, Beijing has launched repeated charm offensives to win its love, but each time to disastrous effect. The "Individual Visit Scheme" (自由行) was meant to be a gift to Hong Kong. It aimed at reviving the city's economy after the 2003 SARS outbreak with mainland tourist dollars. The scheme backfired, however, when Chinese visitors became the culprits for rising property prices and bumper to bumper traffic. Then came the National and Moral Education debacle. Envisioned as an effort to redesign the school curriculum to instill a sense of patriotism in our children, instead it drove half the city to the streets demanding the brainwashing propaganda be scrapped. Less than a year later, the government announced plans to urbanize the Hong Kong-mainland border in the Northeast. The proposal, which sounded benevolent enough, was met with an equal measure of resistance and suspicion. What they called "cross-border integration" sounded to us more like "Sinofication." It appears that each time China takes a step forward, China-Hong Kong relations take two steps back.

But we have plenty of reasons to feel squeamish. Signs that Hong Kong is gradually turning "red" are everywhere. Cantonese is increasingly being marginalized by Mandarin, a language spoken by a population nearly 200 times bigger. Traditional Chinese characters – used in Hong Kong and Taiwan – are slowly giving way to China's simplified characters in public signage and advertisements. More and more local television programming, restaurant menus and retail designs cater to mainlanders. Freedom of expression is on the decline, media self-censorship is on the rise. Our way of life is under threat.

While some think the Sinofication of Hong Kong is inevitable, others are prepared to put up a fight. The hawkish ones – mostly young people within that same 18 to 29 demographic – resort to provocation. At every street rally and anti-government demonstration, they bring out the old colonial flag bearing the Union Jack. The sole purpose is to taunt and offend the Chinese leadership up north. Their message is clear: We hate you so much that we miss the white imperialists! Pretty hurtful stuff.

Clinging to the colonial years

If someone hates his country, he can emigrate and never return. If he loathes his parents, he can cut them out of his life and adopt a different name. A person can change his nationality, his name and even his sex. But what happens if a city experiences an identity crisis? Nearly two decades after the handover, Hong Kong is more lost and isolated than ever. Its future looks murky; its sense of self is fractured. Our ability to articulate who we are and defend what we stand for has taken on an unprecedented urgency. For if we do nothing, Hong Kong will lose its individuality and become just another mainland city. The taxi dispatcher is right: there is no lost and found department for one's identity. We have to work hard to hold on to it.

Martians and Venusians

I

When New York Knicks point guard Jeremy Lin led his team on a seven-game winning streak in the 2012 NBA season, he started something he didn't expect. The so-called "Linsanity" phenomenon catapulted the 23-year-old Taiwanese-American into the national consciousness and captured the imagination of the entire Chinese speaking world. At the same time, Lin's meteoric rise from zero to hero touched off a torrent of public debate on a subject that has hitherto received little attention: the image deficit of the Asian Male.

Lin overcame great odds to be on the court

When asked to comment on Lin's sudden fame, NBA royalty Kobe Bryant said, "His skill level was there from the beginning. It probably just went unnoticed." Kobe was spot on. Until his accidental NBA debut, Lin was underestimated and overlooked. Despite having led his high school team to the California state title, he was routinely snubbed by college recruiters and NBA scouts. Unlike Yao Ming who was revered and reviled as a freak of nature from a foreign country, Lin was written off as just another Asian-American kid from LA. The Knicks wouldn't have given him a shot if it weren't for the fact that their backcourt was decimated by injuries.

If Lin's story sounds familiar, that's because it is happening every day in America. Asian-American men across the country struggle to get noticed and get ahead. From high school hallways and college dorms to the bar room and the board room, the Asian Male is the underdog and the dark horse. He is the wallflower that never gets picked and the spectacled boy who sits at the back of the bus. He is the invisible man.

The absence of positive role models in the mainstream media in America is one reason why Asian American men feel boxed in and left out. Ask anyone in the States to name a famous Asian-American woman and you get the whole list: Lucy Liu, Connie Chung, Lisa Ling, Margaret Cho and, of course, Facebook founder Mark Zuckerberg's wife Priscilla Chan. Now try naming an Asian-American male celebrity. Let's see: Bruce Lee is dead; Jackie Chan is not American and neither is Ken Watanabe. Who is that Korean dude in *Star Trek* again?

Turn on the television and you will find Caucasian male characters in sitcoms and drama series dating Asian women. Ross courted Julie in *Friends* and Dr. Pratt went after Dr. Chen in *ER*. Who goes after Asian-American men? Well, there are no Asian-American men on television! When an Asian male finally beats the odds and lands a part, the character is predictably nerdy, unattractive and always single. Written into the script for racist comic relief, the role is short lived and rarely has more than a few lines. No example is more poignant that the Raj Koothrappali character in CBS's hit comedy *The Big Bang Theory*. Raj, an astrophysicist from India with many feminine tendencies, is so shy around women that for six full seasons of the show he was physically unable to talk to them without the aid of alcohol. His sister Priya, on the other hand, is a desirable, eloquent and self-assured vixen who was relentlessly pursued by the show's lead male character. Coincidence? I think not.

Asian men don't fare much better on the big screen either. Little has changed since Mickey Rooney played Holly Golightly's Japanese neighbor in *Breakfast at Tiffany's* and shouted "Missa Gorightry" at Audrey Hepburn. When Chow Yun-fat and Jet Li were cast as leading men in *Replacement Killers* and *Romeo Must Die* during Hollywood's brief Asian Boom in the late 1990s, neither actor got close to even kissing their non-Asian love interests, let alone getting to second or third base. They were Hollywood's original 40-year-old virgins long before Steve Carell. The unsexing of the Asian man, according to Japanese-American writer David Mura, makes him the "eunuch of America." It goes some way to explain why white-man-Asian-woman relationships outnumber Asian-man-white-woman ones by a wide margin.

Those who hope that the Jeremy Lin sensation will shatter cultural stereotypes in America are in for a big disappointment. We cringe in horror when we hear the audience heckle him and shout racial slurs from the stands. In the same week that a Fox Sports columnist made a quip about Lin's penis size on Twitter, an ESPN news anchor used the headline "Chink in the Armor" after the Knicks lost a game. Both offenders were quick to apologize but the damage was done. It seems all too clear that in America, the Home of the Brave and Land of the Free, old stereotypes die hard and racial prejudices live on. It will take many more Jeremy Lins before Asian men won't need to scream and shout to get noticed and bend over backward to get ahead. Until then, these invisible men will continue to go dateless on prom night, get passed over for job promotions and find themselves defending their body image when the dirty jokes inevitably turn on them.

In Hong Kong, where Asians are on their home turf and male role models abound, Asian men go about their lives free from racial stigmas. No one here would jeer "wonton soup" or "sweet and sour pork" at a Chinese or tell him to "take a boat back to China."

Alas, the Asian men's blues know no geographical bounds, and they – or should I say, we – in Hong Kong have our fair share of image deficit despite our home court advantage. The stereotypes and prejudices attached to Chinese men in Hong Kong are not so much racial as they are *social*. Even though our woes are not nearly as venomous as those facing our brothers in America, they are every bit as real.

The stereotypical Hong Kong man is one who works too hard and knows too little. Compared to his female counterpart, he is clueless about art, music, wine and culture. At work, he is out-smarted by women who speak better English and pay more attention to detail. In the romance department, he is out-maneuvered by divas who have higher EQs and are savvier at head games. The stereotype has a name. In the local vernacular, an "apartment male" (宅男) is a home grown Hong Kong man who locks himself in his bedroom and licks his wounds in front of the computer.

To shake the apartment male stereotype, many Hong Kong men go out of their way to find a hobby to make themselves more interesting. That's why they take up the saxophone or learn to scuba dive. Photography and martial arts classes in the city are filled with men in their 30s and 40s looking to build a better self-image. But once the class ends or their attention span runs out, whichever comes first, many retreat to their comfort zone and delight in being left alone with their video game consoles.

The Asian male has an image problem. Having spent half my life in North America and the other half in Hong Kong, I know what it's like to live with preconceived notions in both environments. Over time, we have developed a range of defense mechanisms to cope. While some adopt a different lifestyle and carefully craft a new persona, others choose not to change a thing and tune out mainstream society altogether. Still others strike a happy balance between the two extremes and believe that their inner strength will prevail. They have faith that even though the arc of history is long, it will always bend toward justice. The truth will one day vindicate them. Until then, being good at math and spending an occasional night reading comic books won't hurt anyone.

II

From New York and Tokyo to Shanghai and Hong Kong, single women in big cities around the world are united in their gripe about being luckless in love. Educated, intelligent and financially independent, they excel in everything in life except for the one thing that really matters to them: finding Mr. Right. The twin goals of marriage and motherhood – things that women a generation ago took for granted – have become ever elusive. Cinderella and Snow White might have had their fair share of heartache before they got hitched, but all the chores and poisoned apples in Fairyland pale in comparison to the blood, sweat and tears of the single woman in the real world. For who wants to die alone in a musty apartment with five cats and a ball of yarn?

Ever since *Sex and the City* glamorized the life of the bachelorette, being female, single and over 35 has never been so cool. But behind the martinis and witty one-liners, the girl power and lipstick feminism, is the lingering fear of spinsterhood. Nowhere in the world is that fear more acute than in Asia, where single women past the ripe age of 30 are viewed with suspicion and pity. Whereas we think of men who delay marriage as free spirits who do so by choice, women who stay single are social rejects who do so by circumstance. The Japanese call them *makeinu* (敗犬), or literally "loser dogs," for having failed in their God-given mission. In the Chinese speaking world, the term *sheng nu* (剩女) or "leftover girls" is now part of our everyday parlance. As if these social stigmas aren't harsh enough, single women in Asia must fend off constant nagging from parents and relatives. At every family gathering, they can count on a nosy aunt to rip their hearts out in front of everyone with that biting question: "Still single, dear?"

A "leftover girl" striking a cute pose

In Hong Kong, women outnumber men by a growing margin. According to the latest government census, there are 876 men for every 1,000 women in the city, down from 960 just a decade ago. Within the age group of 25 to 44, the gender imbalance is even more stark: 725 men for every 1,000 women. Scientists are looking at whether chemical additives used in daily products, like plasticizer and Bisphenol-A, have something to do with the low male birth rate in the city. Meanwhile, the economic reality of the New China is skewing the sex ratio in Hong Kong even more by causing a flight of male professionals to the north. The migration of local men to the mainland in search of better job opportunities drains the already shallow pool of eligible bachelors. With fewer chairs in the room, more women are left standing when the music stops.

Besides facing tough competition for a slim picking of men, women in Hong Kong have an image problem. The phrase "princess syndrome" was coined to describe the behavioral pattern of a subset of local girls. Deluded into thinking that they are the center of the universe, the stereotypical Hong Kong female is a high maintenance brat who demands constant attention and expensive gifts on every occasion. She doesn't lift a finger and has her man wrapped around it instead. Since every ugly stepsister thinks of herself as Cinderella, the princess is dateless on Friday nights and doesn't understand why. As frustration turns into despair, her cynicism grows and mood swings intensify, dragging her deeper down the rabbit hole.

As their biological clock continues to tick like a time bomb, single women – especially those approaching the upper end of their childbearing years – must race against time before they turn into spoiled milk or yesterday's news. They have little choice but to lower standards and manage expectations. The notion that a white knight will come along and sweep them off their feet is long forgotten. While some begin to go for much older men and compromise on the trifecta of masculinity: hair, height and wealth, others hang up their boots and prepare to stay single for good. The second group is telling themselves that marriage is only one of many ways to achieve happiness in life. Friends, family and the freedom to do things that married women cannot are as good as the white picket fence. They choose spinsterhood over a loveless marriage or a nasty divorce.

I'm no dating expert and I don't have any advice to offer single women. What I do have is a few observations I've made over the years watching my female friends lumber on the arduous road to happily ever after. They struggle not for a lack of good looks or a kind heart, but rather because they expect a relationship to solve every problem in their lives. With so much pressure weighing on them, they have a tendency to turn a first date into a job interview or a symposium on marriage and family planning. It is not a mystery why guys don't ask them out on a second date.

So what is a single woman to do? I say do what single men do: get out there and go to places where you can meet a maximum number of people, whether it is a bar, a cooking class or a marathon. Hiding at home for fear of rejection is the worst thing you can do when you are trying to beat the clock. When you finally meet someone interesting and interested, try to keep an open mind. Instead of focusing on his flaws, look for things you may like about him. While he may not be Prince Charming, chances are you are no Cinderella either. Remember, boys read fairy tales too.

遠 大 前 程

Great Expat'ations

Joanna and Jeremy Sandler, together with their daughter Flora, relocated to Hong Kong from New York City three months ago. Joanna is a 36-year-old in-house counsel at an investment bank. Jeremy, a year older than his wife, is an architect. Joanna and I spent years in the trenches at the same law firm in Manhattan, and the three of us have been friends for well over a decade. It was surreal to see old faces suddenly pop up in Hong Kong – it felt out of context.

Last Saturday, I paid the Sandlers a visit in their new home in Ho Man Tin. It took the couple over a month to find an apartment they both liked. However, it didn't take them long to notice a few things about Hong Kong.

Joanna's first observation was predictably about the air. The young mother had been coughing non-stop ever since she came down with the flu eight weeks earlier. I told her the culprit is roadside emissions, 40% of which come from double deckers. That's why the sky is always somewhere between a grayish blue and mauve. "If it makes you feel any better," I said, "we all suffer from one respiratory problem or another. It could be worse – you could be living in Beijing."

Pollution is the first thing that many newcomers notice. The second thing is the property market. I was wondering when the other shoe would drop when Joanna uttered the most dreaded word in Hong Kong: rent. She said they were priced out of Hong Kong Island and had to settle for a three-bedroom in Kowloon. I told her "settled" was not the right word because 1,500 square feet is three times what a typical family gets and Ho Man Tin is a fancy neighborhood. "It'd better be," the lawyer replied. "A third of our monthly pay goes to the apartment!" "Welcome to Hong Kong," I said. If she thinks the rent is high now, wait till the 14-month rent freeze clause in the lease expires and the landlord asks for a 30% increase.

She then moved on to the topic of clothes. Joanna can't find anything that fits her here. She isn't a heavy woman and yet shopping in Hong Kong makes her feel like a blue whale. Joanna keeps a running list of things to buy next time she goes back to New York: dryer sheets, children's books and clothes *not* made for petite Asian women.

It was Jeremy's turn to vent. At six-foot-three, he bumps his head on low hanging signs above the sidewalk all the time. The overhead hand grip on the subway train bounces off his chin like a boxing speed bag. As a result, he is always mildly concussed in Hong Kong. "It's like that in Japan too," I said half-heartedly, for I was lost in my own thoughts wondering how I had gone from always being the shortest person in an elevator in New York to being one of the tallest here. There are many things I miss about living in the Big Apple – Central Park, museums, blue skies – but feeling like I was chopped at the knees is not one of them.

Next, the architect grumbled about schools. Flora doesn't know Chinese and so she can't attend local schools. The waiting list at any of the two dozen international schools is so long that the four-year-old has better odds winning the Powerball. Then there is the sky high tuition, the debentures and the parent interviews. "It's a complete nightmare," Jeremy shook his head. "Didn't your government think of this? It's as if the city doesn't want us here." But we do. We just aren't very good at planning ahead.

"Domestic help is wonderful though," Jeremy changed his tone. A smile bloomed on his face like a daisy on a summer day. "I can't believe we can actually go to the movies and not worry about feeding Flora or taking her to the bathroom. Joanna and I haven't gone out by ourselves for years."

Flora heard her name and put down the iPad. She wanted to chime in with an observation of her own. "People point their fingers at me," she pouted, "and then they call me fat." Flora is nowhere near fat; she just happens to have very pinchable cheeks.

"That's our way of saying you are cute and cuddly," I defended my people. But the four-year-old was right: political correctness is not generally practiced in Hong Kong. Words like "fat," "old," "ugly" and "retarded" are thrown around like daggers in a circus act. It is socially acceptable, for instance, for perfect strangers to address a large man as *fei lo* (肥佬; fat man) to his face. We use it as a term of endearment and no one is supposed to get offended.

"You guys look settled in," I changed the subject. "Look, you've even got cable!"

"Oh my god," Joanna's eyes suddenly narrowed. "I spent three hours on the phone with the PCCW guy just to cancel a channel I never agreed to buy. He kept saying 'Sorry, ma'am' to every question I asked. I thought service in Asia was supposed to be good." It *is* good, but only if the requests are covered in the training manual. Anything outside the script uniformly meets with an apology. And please don't expect us to speak English *and* think at the same time.

On the subject of speaking English, the Sandlers have a sneaking suspicion that because they don't speak Cantonese, taxi drivers routinely take them for a ride and street vendors gouge them like they were tourists in Cairo. Jeremy had a mailbox key made at a hardware store the other day and paid HK$35 (US$4.50) for it. "I bet if you had gone," he gave me a nudge, "they would have charged you HK$5." That prompted me to teach him the Cantonese expression "seafood prices" (海鮮價). We use it in situations where we have no idea how much something is supposed to cost – like ordering a steamed grouper at a Chinese restaurant or taking the car to the mechanic – we just pay what the bill says. The only difference between Jeremy and me is that everything he buys feels like a steamed fish.

Complaints and suspicions aside, there are many reasons why people like the Sandlers uproot their lives and travel across the ocean to be here. Hong Kong has it all: jobs, convenience and breakneck efficiency. *The Economist* conducted a survey several years ago and found Hong Kong to be the most livable place in the world. The rankings were based on factors like infrastructure, safety, connectivity, culture, environment and education. People in other cities like Singapore and Shanghai, which were ranked 22nd and 33rd in the survey, cried foul and disputed the methodology. Even folks in Hong Kong were surprised by the results. Whether you believe that an intensely personal question like a city's livability can be reduced to a single index, there is one thing that everyone can agree on: expats do love Hong Kong.

And Hong Kong loves them right back. The city craves anything imported: chocolates, jeans, cars, music and even the people. Especially the people. What's not to like about them? Most expatriates are highly skilled professionals in their moneymaking prime. People like the Sandlers are sent here to move up the corporate ladder or head up a regional office. These well-heeled foreigners over-tip and order expensive wine at restaurants. They take taxis everywhere and buy real DVDs. In return, the city bends over backwards to make their lives as easy as possible (despite hiccups like air quality and schools). They get an ID card in a week and permanent residency in seven years. Hong Kong is a playground and admission is free!

At the same time, expats are also highly mobile and notoriously capricious. Like canaries in a coal mine, they are first to smell the first sign of trouble. Unlike the caged birds, however, they will pack up and leave on a moment's notice, which makes them a reliable indicator of a city's long term competitiveness. It also makes their presence a seal of approval. Real estate agents in Hong Kong often tout a neighborhood by the number of foreigners living in it. Local retailers like Giordano and Chow Sang Sang hire only Caucasian models in their advertising campaigns. Anywhere else in the world, not being able to speak the local language would be a serious handicap. Here in Hong Kong, starting a conversation with "Sorry, I don't speak Cantonese" can get you better service.

"So will Flora be learning Chinese in school?" I asked. "And are you two learning it as well?"

Yes and yes, they said. But only Mandarin. Cantonese is unpopular among expats because it is considered neither very useful (the mainland market is a hundred times bigger than ours) nor particularly beautiful (they find Mandarin more melodious). To the untrained ear, Cantonese comes off as harsh and shrill, but that's only because living in Hong Kong subjects one to daily abuses of the language: arguing, cursing and yelling at unwieldy children. They will find Mandarin just as hard on the ears if they move to the mainland and listen to cab drivers scream expletives during rush hours.

Learning Chinese is in vogue

"You don't need Cantonese to get by in Hong Kong," I conceded, "but try to pick up a few sentences anyway."

I gave the Sandlers a few reasons why they should. First, Cantonese is the best deterrence against gouging. Jeremy would have avoided seafood prices at the hardware store had he walked in asking confidently for *"sor see"* (key in Cantonese). Second, service people are more solutions-oriented in their native tongue. Instead of "sorry, ma'am," the cable guy at PCCW might have told Joanna something like: "That seems strange to me too... Let me find out if there's something else I can do." Third, Cantonese is a highly expressive language and we use it to poke fun at everything. Life would be much richer if Joanna could eavesdrop on the animated conversation at the dim sum restaurant or if Jeremy could understand why his local colleagues snickered when he wore a green hat to work on a casual Friday. Knowing Cantonese is the only way to sink one's teeth into Hong Kong life.

But maybe the Sandlers don't want to. Expatriates are a funny sort. As if they know they are living on borrowed time, they keep the city at arm's length. They hang out at bars and private clubs, and only in Central and Wanchai. Causeway Bay and Tsim Sha Tsui are too crowded for comfort, and Mongkok is too parochial for their taste. There are exceptions of course, but most expats manage to stay agnostic about local politics and social issues. They stop noticing the old ladies who push heavy carts up D'Aguilar Street and the 1.3 million people living below the poverty line. I suppose if you are sipping champagne in business class, you don't really want to know what goes on in coach.

I got up to thank Joanna and Jeremy for inviting me over. At the door, I turned around to give Flora a hug and took another look around the apartment. In the diamond shaped living room, toys and storybooks were strewn all over the old parquet floor. The dutiful helper brought out a tray and started clearing tea cups and saucers. On the other side of the windows guarded by aluminum bars, a sliver of Victoria Harbour peers between two tall buildings, making good on the real estate broker's promise of an ocean view. The scene made me think that expats aren't that different from us after all. Not three months into their new lives, the Sandlers were well on their way to becoming true Honkies.

One more thing, for those of you who don't speak Cantonese, "to wear a green hat" is to be cheated on by one's wife. That's why local men never put anything green on their heads.

女傭在港

Maid in Hong Kong

I

Few symbols of colonialism are more universally recognized than the live-in maid. From the British trading post in Bombay to the cotton plantation in Mississippi, images abound of the olive-skinned domestic worker buzzing around the house, cooking, cleaning, ironing and bringing ice cold lemonade to her masters who keep grumbling about the summer heat. It is ironic that, for a city that cowered under colonial rule for a century and a half, Hong Kong should have the highest number of maids per capita in Asia. In our city of contradictions, neither a modest income nor a shoebox apartment is an obstacle for local families to hire a domestic helper and to free themselves from chores and errands.

A familiar sight in Hong Kong every Sunday

On any given Sunday or public holiday, migrant domestic workers carpet every inch of open space in Central and Causeway Bay. They turn parks and footbridges into camping sites with cardboard boxes as their walls and opened umbrellas as their roofs. They play cards, cut hair, sell handicrafts and practice complicated dance routines for upcoming talent contests. It is one of those Hong Kong phenomena that charms tourists and fascinates newcomers. Local citizens, on the other hand, have grown so used to the weekly nuisance that they no longer see it or hear it. When the night falls, the music stops and the crowds disperse. One by one, the fun loving revelers return to their employers' homes for another week of mindless drudgery. The weeks will turn into months, months into years.

In the late 1970s, Hong Kong was experiencing record economic growth and transforming from a manufacturing to a service-based economy. The colonial government found itself facing the twin problems of labor shortage and rising labor costs. In an effort to encourage local women to enter the workforce, the government eased restrictions on migrant workers and brought in the first batch of domestic helpers from the Philippines. In the decades that followed, the number of Filipino maids in the city continued to rise, as more young women followed in the footsteps of their friends and relatives and moved here in search of higher pay and a chance to live overseas. Other South East Asian countries soon caught on and joined in the labor export business. Today, there are roughly 140,000 Filipino domestic helpers in the city, just as many from Indonesia and around 4,000 from Thailand.

Back in the Philippines, women with a college education – who make up the bulk of the migrant workers overseas – make around HK$2,000 (US$260) a month as office clerks. Those who work in a restaurant or a store make about half that amount. The problem is not so much that wages are low but that there is a persistent shortage of jobs. The country's unemployment rate, especially in rural areas, is believed to be far higher than the 7.3% reported by the government.

Here in Hong Kong, these women are offered a steady paycheck, plus free room and board and a roundtrip ticket home once every two years. In exchange, they must leave behind their own family and live a vicarious life in a stranger's home. They must also endure homesickness, loneliness, spousal infidelity, and occasional verbal and even physical abuse by their employers. Fearing reprisals and termination of their employment contracts, domestic helpers keep their mouths shut when they are asked to do things they are not supposed to (such as giving massages and cleaning someone else's apartment) or paid less than the legally required amount. Indeed, the rising popularity of Indonesian maids among local families owes in part to their reputation for being soft-spoken and obliging, and in part to their willingness to accept as much as a 50% discount from the statutory minimum wage.

By law, employers are required to pay their live-in helpers a minimum monthly salary of roughly HK$4,000 (US$500). This amount reflects how much our society values the economic benefit of freeing up a parent from domestic responsibilities to earn a second household income. For the price of a nice family meal or a couple of facials, we get to hold a fellow human being in captivity while we are out in the world making 10, 20 times the salary we pay her. Though much of the city's economic success is built on the backs of these migrant workers, they remain one of the most mispriced commodities in our economy. That's why most *gweilo* employers voluntarily pay their domestic workers more than the legal minimum, starting at HK$5,000 (US$640) and sometimes as high as HK$8,000 (US$1,000).

The pay differential between the two communities is largely unknown and irrelevant to the local population. Most Chinese employers see absolutely nothing wrong with sticking to the legal minimum. There appears to be a simple justification: if they don't like it, they can always take the next boat back to the Philippines! We got a glimpse of that line of reasoning when the government raised the minimum allowable wage by a meager HK$160 (US$20) per month in 2011, an increase of less than 5%. The move was meant to pacify the migrant worker community after the government callously excluded them from the protection of the new minimum hourly wage legislation. Nevertheless, the pay raise prompted unhappy citizens to call in to radio talk shows to complain about the excessive increase and the added financial burden on the middle class. No doubt the callers were already thinking up new ways to work their maids a little harder to make up the difference.

The access to cheap domestic help has altered many aspects of our lives, but no one benefits from it more than our senior citizens. At home, the maid is a 24-hour private nurse who answers their every need, which is especially handy for those who suffer from chronic illnesses like diabetes and kidney disease. Out on the streets, she is a boon companion who takes them to the park, the market and the doctor's office. It is she who gives them mobility and a better quality of life. It warms my heart every time I see a dutiful maid offer her shoulder as a crutch to help a grandmother get off a minibus, a scene lifted straight out of *Driving Miss Daisy*. If it weren't for the help, the old woman may have been cooped up in a small flat staring at a blank wall all day.

I don't have a live-in maid and I have never thought about getting one. Besides finding the idea too colonial, I would probably feel awkward having another person living next to me in such close quarters. Still, every other family in my apartment building seems to have a helper; some even have more than one. Every day I see them walking the family dog or lugging bagfuls of groceries. They hold the door for me and let me get into the elevator before them, always with a smile on their faces. The fact that they would yield to someone they don't even work for reminds me of the social divide that still exists between us and them. More than three decades after their predecessors first arrived in Hong Kong, these migrant workers are still not afforded full membership in our society. Like it or not, these quasi-citizens unflinchingly hold up a mirror to our city and reveal our parsimony and ingratitude to those who have made an immeasurable contribution to our prosperity.

Raquel Nunag contributed research.

II

The Final Court of Appeal handed down the long awaited ruling. The judges were unanimous: migrant workers were not entitled to permanent residency in Hong Kong regardless of the length of their stay. Outside the red brick courthouse, a group of Filipinas stood in a circle. Sobs were audible, tears welled up in their eyes. Years of legal battle were all for naught. The judgment was hardly a surprise, but it still felt like a kick in the stomach.

Not thirty feet away, a different crowd congregated. Cheers and slogans shrieked from a bullhorn. They were members of a self-proclaimed pro-Hong Kong alliance. "Go back to Fee-lip-peen," a Chinese man taunted in bad English. The banners in their hands spelled out a slew of doomsday scenarios: hundreds of thousands of maids would flood our streets, followed by their husbands and children. Social spending would skyrocket, unemployment would soar. The city would fall.

Their demands have fallen on 7 million pairs of deaf ears

One of the protagonists in the high profile lawsuit was Ms. Evangeline Vallejos, a Filipina who had worked in Hong Kong since 1986. The Basic Law, Hong Kong's mini-constitution, guarantees any person the right to apply for permanent residency after he or she has ordinarily resided in the city for seven years; although that didn't stop the Immigration Department from denying Vallejos' application because she is a foreign maid. She sued and the case went all the way to the top court. In the end, the claimant lost on a technicality. The court ruled that Vallejos had not "ordinarily resided" in Hong Kong because her stay was highly restricted, as all migrant workers are required to live with their employers and return to their home countries if their contracts are not renewed. Never mind that Vallejos had worked 18 hours a day, six days a week for 27 years in Hong Kong. Her residence was not only ordinary; it was extraordinary.

Our migrant worker policy has been flawed from the start. It was meant to be a quick fix for our changing economy, but little thought was given to how we could handle the sudden influx of foreign workers. To get a sense of our callousness, look no further than the mayhem on our sidewalks and footbridges every Sunday when helpers get a day off and have nowhere to go. For over 30 years, our government has done nothing to address the issue of space. Not one community center was built for them; not a single empty schoolyard was arranged for their use. In the 1980s, frustrated landlords in Central tried to persuade the squatters to move to underground parking lots. Leaders of the migrant worker community rejected the proposal for a simple reason: they are people, not cars.

Sadly, that's exactly how the city views these migrant workers – we see them as machines. We switch them on in the morning and turn them off at night. Like household appliances, they are expected to be purely functional and devoid of feelings.

Even second class citizens would have been treated with more humanity. For decades, domestic helpers have been asking us the same question: "Why do Hong Kong people dislike us so much?" It is a question that every dual income middle class family with a live-in maid should ask themselves. Here are a few possible answers.

The first is valuation. We measure a domestic worker's contribution at cost instead of replacement value. Priced at around HK$4,000 (US$500) per month, she is worth as much as a monthly parking space or a used computer. It is easy to dismiss parking spaces and old computers. On the other hand, if we were to replace her with a stay-at-home spouse or a local employee, the valuation would increase dramatically. Imagine the cost of hiring a Hong Kong person with cooking, childcare and nursing skills for around the clock care, *if* you could find one at all. And imagine the kind of bidding war if 300,000 households all wanted one in their homes. They could put their HK$4,000 in a pipe and smoke it!

The second reason has to do with that dirty p-word: prejudice. Not all foreigners in Hong Kong are created equal. When we think of Caucasians, we picture well paid professionals who work in Central and live in Midlevels. We roll out the red carpet and reward their seven-year stay with automatic permanent residency. And we use the word "expat" instead of "immigrant" or "foreign worker" to reflect their VIP status.

When we think of Philippine or Indonesian women, on the other hand, all we see is dirty dishes and unmade beds. In our narrow minds, these third world laborers are dark-skinned, uneducated and lazy as a sloth. The idea of having them eat at the same restaurants and work in the same jobs next to us is a hard pill to swallow. Granting them residency would be a blow to our superiority complex.

The third reason is willful blindness. Deep down many of us know that migrant workers have the short end of the stick and that they probably deserve more, but there is no way to help *them* without hurting *us*. We have grown accustomed to their cheap service and no one wants to pay more. We deny them permanent residency because our social resources are limited. So we turn a blind eye to the inconvenient truth, sweep the dirt under the rug and pretend it doesn't exist.

In an unfathomable show of selfishness, our courts, with the overwhelming support of the local population, denied a segment of our society their constitutional right to be citizens alongside us. We shout out to the entire world that Hong Kong, for all its claims to be a world class city, will always choose self-interest over principle, expedience over the rule of law. Ironically, it wasn't so long ago when we were victims of social injustice. Until 1997, we were treated as inferior subjects of a European colony. During the Hong Kong Diaspora, we were immigrants on foreign soil struggling to fit in. How ready we are to inflict upon others what we don't want inflicted on us.

A society is measured not by the success of the rich but how it treats its most vulnerable. To be part of a civilized society is to learn to give and take, live and let live. For if we don't stand up for those in need, we can't expect anyone to stand up for us when the roles reverse. The Vallejos case has given us 300,000 reasons to reflect on what we as a people stand for and what message we are giving our children. As a Hong Konger, I am embarrassed by my own people. And to Ms. Vallejos and her fellow domestic helpers, I want to say I am sorry.

III

When Loretta left the Philippines in the 1980s, she didn't have any training in cooking or housekeeping. What she did have was an eight-year-old son she had to feed back in Quezon City.

Loretta got pregnant when she was 17 and soon thereafter her boyfriend disappeared. Left with no other choice, the single mother – a title she carried in her hometown for eight years like a scarlet letter – turned her child over to his grandmother and headed to Hong Kong in 1983.

In the past 30 years, she has served twelve local Chinese families across the city. The Chans, the Wongs and the Leungs – Loretta has seen it all. For a quarter of a century, she cleaned their apartments, ate in their kitchen and listened to the radio by herself in the maid's quarter. Most of her employers treated her well enough, though none of them ever considered her one of their own. Not once have they invited her to eat with them, watch television with them, or simply have a chat with them. Loretta has heard that back in the day those Chinese maids with their braided queues – "amah" (媽姐) as they were called – often became their employers' best friends and confidants. When it comes to Filipinas, however, a maid is always just a maid. She wonders if the complexion of her skin has something to do with it. Or is it a trust issue? She was told that Chinese people, especially the Cantonese, have problems trusting people, especially those who look and sound different from them.

Speaking of trust, she remembers the Kos. She worked for them for only nine months in the late 1980s. Mrs. Ko wouldn't believe a word her maid said; she never had. That's why Loretta kept Mr. Ko's dirty little secret to herself. Until that fateful moment, she had only heard about these "incidents" at church gatherings;

they were merely urban legends that swirled around within the community.

One Saturday afternoon in 1987 changed all that. While Mrs. Ko was out, her husband summoned Loretta to his bedroom. He patted gently on the bed and signaled her to get closer. The 29-year-old pretended that nothing happened and went back to her ironing in the kitchen. In all, it happened three more times before Mr. Ko finally gave up. Each time he warned her not to say anything to his wife or he would terminate her contract.

The incidents frightened Loretta, for she no longer felt safe sharing an apartment with a man she didn't trust, and with a woman who didn't trust her. More still the incidents angered her. She wasn't angry with Mr. Ko – he was just a sad, sexually frustrated man. She was angry with herself and her country – the Maid Capital of the World whose people were allowed to be humiliated and taken advantage of at will.

Loretta now works for an expat family. The Johnsons treat their 55-year-old helper like an aunt and pay her HK$6,500 (US$830) a month – the most she has made all this time in Hong Kong – plus a plane ticket and pocket money every year to visit her son in Manila. These days when Loretta is home alone, she reads a book or makes small handicrafts that she sells to other churchgoers on Sundays.

Loretta still chuckles when she thinks about some of the silly things that young maids do to kill time when their bosses aren't around: trying on their name brand clothes, putting on their expensive makeup and taking naps in their beds. The more daring ones bring men home – men they meet in those sleazy bars on Lockhart Road – and have a jolly good time. All that, and so much more, observed by the veteran maid day after day for 30 years. New recruits who have just arrived in the city often go to see Loretta, and the reigning matriarch always dispenses the same advice: be patient. "If you let every little thing get to you, you won't last a month in Hong Kong," she tells them before giving them a motherly hug.

Loretta was barely 25 when she came to Hong Kong

Whenever Loretta looks in the mirror, she is reminded of the long way she has come since her wayward teenage years. Three decades of hardship and loneliness have chiseled her face. Despite all the years she has spent in the city, Hong Kong people are still a mystery to her. Why is it that they have everything in life but none of them looks very happy? Back in the Philippines, people live from hand to mouth and yet she hears more laughter in Quezon City than anywhere in Hong Kong.

Still, Loretta adores Hong Kong. Above all, she admires its energy and the people's endless desire to live a better life. By contrast, Filipinos are all too quick to accept the *status quo*, like her son, now 38, who is barely scraping by in Manila and still requires his mother's constant reminder to seek out more from life. If only the two peoples could balance each other out.

*   *   *

Anna hasn't been in Hong Kong very long. The 23-year-old moved to the city less than two years ago. The bustling metropolis is a far cry from Aguso, the sleepy Philippine farming village in the province of Tarlac that she left behind, along with her father, two brothers and a fiancé named James. The young couple got engaged just weeks before she left the country. They knew the perils of a long distance relationship, but they did it anyway. Nothing has to change, they thought. But everything did.

The spirited, college educated Filipina remembers her first day in the city like it was yesterday. Her mother, also a domestic helper in Hong Kong, picked her up from the airport – a blinding stadium of marble floors and steel beams – and took her to the employer's home where they would both work. Anna was luckier than other Filipinas. Most of her friends, or "sisters" as they call each other, arrived in the new city by themselves, only to be greeted by a complete stranger sent by the agency. The unlucky ones were placed with a "terror employer" – that's what they call abusive Chinese families that work their helpers like slaves. Not Anna; she was with her mom. As the Airport Express train quietly zoomed through the jungle of high rise apartment buildings, she actually felt lucky to be a second generation maid.

Every Filipina who leaves her country to become a domestic worker does it for her own reason. For Anna's mother, it was a necessity because her husband lost his job as a tricycle driver after an injury. For young Anna, it was an opportunity to reacquaint herself with her mother who left home when she was only six. Fate has brought them back together. Mother and daughter are now working side by side, sharing a small air-conditionless room in a Midlevels apartment. Although it is good to have mom around, it is not always easy to be treated like a child all over again.

Anna had initially planned to stay for only two years, just long enough to get to know her mother and make a few extra bucks before she went home to James. Her plans were shattered just six months into her new job. Back home, James got into a motorcycle accident and went through multiple surgeries. After months of recuperation, he suddenly broke off the engagement. His change of heart might have something to do with his head injuries, the doctor said. Or was it another woman? Anna would never know, for she was thousands of miles away and couldn't leave the city during the first 18 months of her employment. None of that matters now – it is all in the past. "Life goes on and you must do something for yourself, Anna," her mother nags. "Anna, make as much money as you can and pay back your loans," her mother nags some more.

Yes, the loans – *always* the loans. Before moving to Hong Kong, Anna borrowed money to pay for her trip to Manila to get a work visa – all the people she needed to pay just to get a piece of paper. She also bought new clothes and shoes for the move. Even a maid ought to look good in Hong Kong, her friends told her. After James' accident, Anna took out a loan many times her monthly salary to pay for his surgeries and medication. Even now, every few months her cousins will ask her for money for school or to repair her uncle's tricycle. So she takes out more loans. That's why she doesn't like going back home. Too many relatives expecting too many handouts. She wonders how they all got by before she had this job.

Anna plans to renew her contract when it expires in the summer. There is no reason to go back to Aguso any more. There, people will pull her down like a ton of bricks, both financially and emotionally. "Life goes on and I must do something for myself," she remembers her mother's words. She wants to move to America one day and go back to school. "To do that, I need to make as much money as I can and pay off my loans," she remembers those other words too. All that has happened has made Anna realize what a wise woman her mother is. She has also realized that her mother has enormous grit, because wisdom alone is not enough to get through all those years working far from home, all by herself. Anna feels she has done what she came to Hong Kong to do. She finally knows her mother.

*   *   *

The profiles featured above are based on my interviews with two Filipinas who graciously agreed to have their stories told. During our conversations, their soft voices beat out detailed accounts of their hard lives. The stories are unique to Loretta and Anna, but they are also the stories of the 140,000 Filipinas working in Hong Kong. While each story is a portrait of one, it is a celebration of *everyone*. Their struggles, their dreams and their cheerful nature give them unity, the kind of unity that makes them smile to each other on the streets and turns perfect strangers into instant friends. Their spirit is, and always will be, their greatest strength.

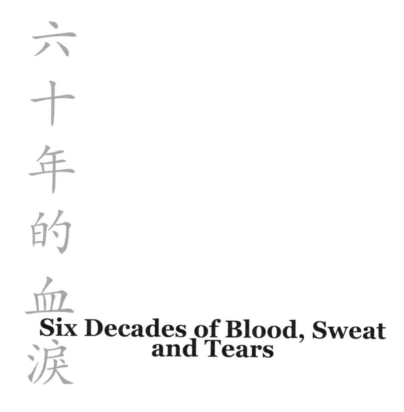

六
十
年
的
血
淚

Six Decades of Blood, Sweat and Tears

My brothers and I visited Beijing a few months ago. The capital city, draped in fall foliage, was magnificent, graceful and brimming with pride. Beneath the veneer of quiet confidence, however, were signs of a city frantically preparing itself for an extravaganza. Every 1 October, the Communist Party goes all out to put on a show to celebrate the anniversary of the founding of the People's Republic. Central to the festivities is a massive military parade, followed by an evening of lavish fireworks and staged performances.

As our taxi sailed past Tiananmen Square, face-lifted for the occasion with giant LCD screens and slogan banners, we spotted convoys of military vehicles docked by the roadside after a day of grueling rehearsals. In a few days, rocket launchers and tanks would rumble down Chang An Avenue (長安街), a scene that most of us associate only with North Korea, Iran and the former Soviet Union. The hoopla surrounding the military review is proof that the Chinese government, despite all the economic progress it has made, still believes that a country's strength is measured by the range of its missiles.

At dinner, my brothers and I washed down Peking duck with Great Wall cabernet, making no bones about mixing food with politics as we looked back on six decades of Communist rule.

* * *

The history of Modern China, at least the first half of it when Mao Zedong was at the helm, is nothing short of a horror story. To this day, however, the Politburo continues to defend Mao's grisly legacy. The Chairman's portrait is still hung high at Tiananmen Square and his embalmed body is on public display in a creepy mausoleum in the heart of the capital. To keep the mythology alive, state propagandists have deified Mao as the Great Helmsman, a Nietzschean *Übermensch* of sorts. They conveniently brush aside the "few mistakes" he made as teachable moments for a fledgling republic. For those of us who are less susceptible to propaganda, however, those few mistakes are all we remember of the Chairman.

In the dog days of summer 1958, Mao launched the most ambitious national experiment of his reign – an economic program that made Franklin D. Roosevelt's New Deal look like child's play. Designed to fast track China's industrialization, the Great Leap Forward diverted tens of millions of farm workers to backyard steel production, leaving crops to rot in the fields and filling houses with useless lumps of pig iron made from farming tools. As a result of one man's bad idea, an estimated 30 million peasants starved to death in history's worst manmade disaster, 40 times the number who died in Ireland's Potato Famine in the 1840s and five times the number killed in the Holocaust.

Red guards in a model play

Horrific as the death toll was, the Great Leap Forward paled in comparison to the unfathomable terror of the Cultural Revolution. After his many failed economic policies, Mao needed to regain his grip on power. In 1966, the Chairman launched a mass social-political movement, carried out primarily by a legion of hypnotized youth called the Red Guards. What started as a political maneuver to purge his rivals quickly spun out of control. For eleven years, the entire country trembled in fear of domestic terrorism. Anyone labeled a "bourgeois" or "capitalist" was likely to be tortured, exiled or killed. Students turned in their teachers, children blew the whistle on their parents. Books were burned, temples were leveled, and anything of any cultural value was destroyed. By 1976, the total destruction of society was complete and 3,500 years of history were undone.

The country began to turn around when Deng Xiaoping took over following Mao's death in 1976. Realizing that endless class struggles and cults of personality would do nothing to get China out of its rut, Deng initiated a series of market-oriented reforms, making China one of the fastest growing economies in the world and earning widespread approval for the regime even among its critics. Just when things started to look up for the republic, however, the flicker of hope was snuffed out at Tiananmen Square, where hundreds of student protesters lost their lives to tanks and rifles. If not for the blood on his hands through action or inaction during that fateful summer, Deng might even have been worthy of a Nobel Peace Prize for bringing stability to a people so thoroughly ravaged by previous leaders. Students of Chinese history know all too well that good times rarely last. On 4 June, 1989, reality hit us in the head like a sledgehammer. Such is the grim destiny of the Middle Kingdom.

*   *   *

Back in the hotel room, I was eager to post my Beijing pictures on Facebook, only to discover that the social networking website, along with Twitter, YouTube and Blogger, were all blocked. I instinctively looked over my shoulders to see if anyone was watching me, suddenly overcome by a feeling of vulnerability. I abandoned my now useless computer and walked over to the window to admire the stunning view of the CCTV Headquarters, nicknamed *da kucha* (大褲衩; literally, big panties) for its curious shape. Next to it was the north annex torched by a fire caused by unauthorized fireworks in 2009. The steel carcass, now completely covered in rust, was left standing years after the fire, as authorities tried to downplay the blunder by insisting that the structure was salvageable. Both the Internet firewall and the burned tower are bitter reminders that, six decades on, China still has a long way to go before it starts acting like the rest of the developed world. On every 1 October, the world's second largest economy has as much to celebrate as it does to reflect on.

蝗
蟲
天
下

The Eighth Plague

I

"They shall cover the face of the land, so that no one can see the land. They shall eat what little you have, including every tree that grows in the field. They shall fill your houses and those of your officials – something neither your fathers nor your grandfathers have ever seen from the day they settled in this land."

– Exodus, 10:5-6.

The plague of locusts, according to the Old Testament, was the eighth calamity that God inflicted upon Egypt to cower Pharaoh into freeing the enslaved Israelites. 2,600 years later, the menacing insect has crawled its way into the 21st Century lexicon in Hong Kong and is now a popular racial slur to refer to the ubiquitous mainland tourists in the city.

It all began in 2003 when the Individual Visit Scheme was introduced to relax travel restrictions on Chinese nationals visiting Hong Kong. Since then, our comrades have been gushing through the border and doubling in number every few years. Tour buses now take up entire lanes on busy thoroughfares and release hordes of visitors into shopping malls and amusement parks. What started as an economic stimulus, however, has become a lightning rod for cross border tension. It appears that the city has gotten more than it had bargained for and that the "red dollar," which topped HK$240 billion (US$30 billion) in 2014, can be too much of a good thing.

To get a sense of how unwelcome these *personas non grata* are, look no further than the hundreds of cell phone videos posted by Hong Kong people on YouTube. The clips depict misbehaving visitors flouting local customs and rules. They have been caught spitting, jumping queues, and eating messy food on public transport. The most egregious cases involve young children urinating or even defecating into trash cans or roadside gutters. Even in upscale locales like the Four Seasons lobby or the Landmark mall, they can be heard hawking phlegm and belching like an Italian baritone. So far, phone cam shaming has been our only weapon against this travesty of human decency. These grainy videos give visual evidence that mainlanders are uncivilized *nouveau riche* who invade, devour and multiply like their namesake insect.

Wherever the swarm settles, from busy shopping areas to border towns in the New Territories, the locusts pillage the area's luxury goods and everyday supplies. They empty shelves and bid up prices for local residents. Entire neighborhoods are being transformed to meet their insatiable appetite for gold watches and skincare products. Near the Lo Wu border control, corner stores and noodle houses have been evicted to make way for pharmacies that sell baby formula to day trippers from nearby Shenzhen.

That's how they roll

The locusts' destructive path extends beyond the realm of retail. Mainland visitors come to Hong Kong with different intentions: while most of them head straight to the malls, others have far bigger plans in mind. Using their new found wealth, opportunistic investors wager on the city's real estate market and snatch up apartment units by the block. They dry up supply and make it even more difficult for local families to afford new homes. In the meantime, pregnant women rush to the emergency room to give birth, all for a piece of paper that guarantees their children permanent residency in Hong Kong. In response to a mounting public outcry, the government has banned hospitals from treating mainland mothers. Still, many fear that the tens of thousands of babies – or the nymphs if you will – who made it through to the delivery room before the ban will put a strain on our school system and job market when they grow up.

Mainlanders drive us crazy but keep us afloat. We can't stand them, and yet we can't live without them. So is that it? Are we innocent victims who must cower to the new rich like old Pharaoh to God's merciless plagues? Before we get too complacent with the locust metaphor, we should challenge the assumptions underlying it.

First, we assume that *all* mainlanders behave the same way. We forget the first lesson on racism: the fallacy of generalization. For every misbehaving Ugly Chinese, there are many more who act just like you and me. We don't notice the well-behaved majority because they simply aren't very noticeable. Applying sweeping stereotypes to an entire group is convenient but unfair. We know because we have been on the receiving end of prejudice. Westerners often jump to conclusions about us based on the behavior of a few. One person forgetting to turn off his phone during a concert is enough for them to shake their heads and say, "These Hong Kong people are unbelievable!"

Second, we assume that mainland tourists and their money are the root of all evil. We never once pause to think that the fault lies with those who make the rules: our government. Hong Kong is a free market, and Chinese tourists are paying customers as good as the next. If we want to give priority to the local population, whether for housing, health care or consumer goods, it is incumbent on our own policymakers to pass the necessary measures. Instead of blaming bureaucrats who are asleep at the switch, we point our fingers at an easy target: the foreigners.

Mainlanders are like any other tourists: they come to Hong Kong looking for a good time instead of trouble. The majority of them try to do the right thing, although they don't always know how and the possibility of committing an inadvertent *faux pas* is magnified by their sheer number. So far, local media and politicians have done little to reverse the misconceptions. On the contrary, many of them are fanning the mass hysteria to sell newspapers and win political points. If left unaddressed, however, cross border tension will boil over, like the way Peking University professor Kong Qingdong (孔慶東) responded to the locust slur by retaliating in kind, calling Hong Kong people "running dogs" who wag their tails to their former British masters. If we find Mr. Kong's animal metaphor preposterous and juvenile, imagine how the mainlanders feel about ours.

II

Dear Hong Kong People,

My name is Wang Li. I'm one of the 18,000 mainland Chinese students and professionals who have made your city our new home. We call ourselves "gang piao" in Mandarin, because we're drifters who are just passing through and never quite belong.

I know how you feel about us, or I should say "them." You call Chinese tourists "locusts," I know. I don't think the comparison is fair, though I understand your frustration. I come from Ningbo, a seaport south of Shanghai. Ningbo people feel the same way when out-of-towners, especially tourists from northern China, come to our city on big holidays. We get annoyed by them too.

I seldom go to Causeway Bay and Tsim Sha Tsui for that reason. Whenever I sense their presence around me, I will switch to English or Cantonese. I don't want to be guilty by association, even though I feel I already am – since most of you can't tell the difference between us and them. These tourists, they don't mean to be rude, you see. They don't get in line because it never occurs to them they should. In China, if you're too polite, you'll never get on a bus or sit down at a restaurant. Also, they speak loudly because they are excited about being in Hong Kong. It's the first time for many of them to be abroad. You remember the first time you got on an airplane or stood in front of the Eiffel Tower?

I was 19 years old when I came here. I was a first year university student and I just wanted to blend in. Within the first month, I got rid of all the clothes I brought from Ningbo and bought new ones. I spent nearly $3,000 on a wallet because I was told that I should have at least one expensive thing on me. Even though I'm not nearsighted, I got myself a pair of black frame eyeglasses that I saw everyone in Hong Kong wear. My parents hardly recognized me when I went home to Ningbo the first summer.

I paid close attention to the way Hong Kong people behave. I tried to use the same words you use and eat the same food you eat. I learned to stand at least two feet from people to give them personal space. I took careful notes so I wouldn't stand out. I didn't want to get a funny nickname like some of my mainland classmates did. I wanted to be called just Wang Li.

Fitting in wasn't easy, but thankfully I didn't have to do it alone. There are many online communities for us gang piao to share survival tips. We also organize social events and offer free Cantonese classes. It's important for us to learn your language, you see. It's the best self-defense. Cantonese is not hard for Mandarin speakers – we just need to put in the time. I would watch Hong Kong movies and listen to Canto pop. I still have an accent, but my Cantonese is good enough for me to get by and chat with sales people. Some of my mainland friends don't speak a word of it. I tell them if after a year they still can't name all the MTR stations between Central and Tin Hau in Cantonese, then they have no one but themselves to blame for feeling like an outsider.

This is my sixth year living in Hong Kong. I will be getting my permanent residence next year and become a Hong Kong resident. Once in a while, I still get what I call a "Hong Kong moment." I get the occasional rude waiter who will serve everyone else before he will serve me. I still get asked: "Why do you people squat in public?" and "Why do you people poison your babies with toxic milk powder?" I mean, there are 1.3 billion people in China and there are all kinds of people doing all kinds of things every day. I don't think the idea of "you people" exists when you're talking about a fifth of the world's population.

A lot of Hong Kong people also think that all gang piao are here because of family connections. You think all of us are "princelings." You see, most of us come from middle class families. My father is a university professor. My friends' parents are accountants and engineers. We're not wealthy by your standards, but our parents work hard and they save money to send us overseas. We are not sons and daughters of high ranking officials who take bribes and drive red Ferraris. So please don't believe everything your newspapers and magazines tell you.

My friends and I try to understand where the prejudice comes from. Many of them think you're threatened by us because cities like Shanghai and Shenzhen are overtaking Hong Kong. The renminbi is now worth more than the Hong Kong dollar. I don't agree with them. I believe what I said about China also applies to Hong Kong. I mean, there are 7 million people in the city and there are all kinds of people doing all kinds of things here. We can't get too excited about what a few people think or say about us.

The truth is: I love Hong Kong. Hong Kong people are so ambitious and work so hard. You make rules and you actually follow them. And the freedom! I can go to a bookstore and read whatever I want. I can go on the Internet and say anything I want. I'm proud to be living and working in Hong Kong. I know my family in Ningbo feels the same way. Every time Ba and Ma talk about me in front of their friends, they call me their "baby in Hong Kong."

My parents ask me how long I plan on staying here, and I tell them I don't know. I tell them Hong Kong is a practical city. The Cantonese don't seem interested in much else other than making money and buying things. Everything is so expensive here – which is partly "my people's" fault, I know. Anyway, I don't envy Hong Kong people. I don't think I can live here forever.

Unfortunately, I can't go back to the mainland either. I mean I can, but I don't want to. China is no place to raise children, you see. Everyone in the country, including children, are part of a big act that has gone on for over 60 years now. When I was in kindergarten in Ningbo, the well-behaved kids were the ones who praised the Party and wore little red handkerchiefs around their necks. In high school, we took history and political science classes to learn why we should follow the State's direction. Stability is always the most important thing. Of course everybody knows it's nonsense. Everybody just plays along, like children in America who pretend they believe in

Santa Claus just to make their parents happy. I don't want my children to grow up in a place like that.

I hope to move to Canada or Australia one day. I'm saving as much as possible so that I can start a family somewhere else after I leave Hong Kong. I won't return to Ningbo to be with my Ba and Ma, you see. I will only be able to visit them like a tourist. I don't know where I belong any more – not my hometown and certainly not Hong Kong. Thinking that makes me want to cry.

I'm writing this open letter to you because these are all the things I want you to know. I also want to say thank you for everything your city has given me. Every day I spend in Hong Kong is a gift. These gifts will stay with me forever. I wish all the mainland tourists who come here could experience what I've experienced and see what I've seen. I wish they knew what it's like to finally be able to breathe. A single breath in the free world is worth more than any gold watch or handbag they bring home. I'm sure of that.

Wang Li

Gao Wei and Richard Sha contributed research.

沒英雄的城市

A Heroless City

Earlier this year, tens of thousands of people flocked to the Times Square shopping center in Causeway Bay. It wasn't the summer sale or the grand opening of a new flagship store. It was the 10th anniversary of the death of Leslie Cheung, one of the most beloved Canto pop singers of all time. A three-story high bust of Cheung stood in the middle of the mall's atrium surrounded by a sea of fans. Some of them were visibly emotional, while others lamented the abrupt end to a shining career. Not since Bruce Lee had any celebrity been able to elicit such an outpouring of grief from the city.

Every country worships its heroes. As Whitney Houston famously put it in her 1986 self-help anthem, "everybody needs someone to look up to." When the heroes fall – think of the assassinations of John F. Kennedy and John Lennon – they take a piece of our hearts with them and leave the world a darker place. In the age of public catharsis, the deaths of cultural icons like Princess Diana, Steve Jobs and Nelson Mandela draw millions of mourners. We remember where we were and what we were doing when we heard the bad news. These days, each time Stephen Hawking checks into the hospital, we wonder if we can stomach another heartbreak of global proportions.

That takes me to an office lunch I had recently. There were five of us at the table: Robert, an Englishman from Sussex; Alex, an American who relocated from L.A. six months ago; and three Hong Kong natives, Tim, Brenda and I. Robert brought up the subject of Margaret Thatcher and the way her death had drawn supporters and opponents in equal numbers to streets across the UK. It didn't take long for the discussion to come back to our city.

"Who do you think would draw the biggest crowd in Hong Kong if he or she were to die tomorrow?" I asked.

"Chris Patten?" Robert suggested.

"Chris who?" Alex asked, while Tim and Brenda shook their heads in unison. The former British governor of Hong Kong is well liked, but flowers and condolence cards from us? Not likely.

"Jackie Chan," Alex cheered. "Everybody *loves* Jackie Chan!"

Tim and I rushed to set the record straight, but I beat him to it.

"Jackie Chan might have been popular 20 years ago," I explained. "He's a social pariah now. He can't stop putting his foot in his mouth." I was referring to the actor-comedian's infamous remark that Chinese people needed to be "controlled."

"Li Ka-shing," Brenda offered, confident that the richest man in Hong Kong would be a safe choice.

This time I let Tim handle the rebuttal. "Li is just as loathed," he said. "Protesters drew fangs on his face during the recent dock workers' strike."

A five-way discussion then followed, but we failed to reach a consensus.

"So, are there no heroes in this city?" Alex ended the debate with a rhetorical question.

My colleague's conclusion plunged me into deep thought. Alex couldn't possibly be right, because every country has its heroes and our city is, at least I hope, no exception. If that's the case, then why was it so difficult for us to come up with even one name?

I decided to get to the bottom of it. To find out which public figures have reached hero-dom, I first need to know who the candidates are. In Hong Kong, there are three categories of celebrities: tycoons, politicians and entertainers. Elsewhere in the world, writers and artists would have made the list as well. But this is Hong Kong after all, and we are not supposed to have any famous writers or artists!

Let's start with the first category: the super rich. Hong Kong is often called an economic city because money talks and those who have lots of it shout. Property, textile and shipping magnates used to be worshipped like deities. Li Ka-shing was famously crowned "Superman" for his Midas touch.

But that is no longer the case. Among the world's wealthiest economies, Hong Kong now has one of the highest Gini coefficients, a widely used measure of income inequality. The yawning gap between the rich and the poor has been blamed on the top 0.01% of society, turning tycoons into public enemies. Being a billionaire has never been so uncool.

The same goes for politicians. In the post-handover era, the constant threat of Sinofication has made us suspicious of anyone who holds a government office. In our minds, the ruling elite are sellouts who have sold their souls to Communist China. Far from being respected, they are lucky if protesters don't burn them in effigy at the annual 1 July civil rights protest.

What about the few good men like Martin Lee and Audrey Eu who hold the line and defend our rights? These day, career politicians who spend their lives climbing the greasy pole find it hard to please everyone. A single misstep can undo years of good work. Two years ago, the death of "Uncle" Szeto Wah, a lifelong teachers' union leader and activist, drew only a modest crowd to his funeral because of a political spat that split his allies and tarnished his legacy. In politics, the line between heroism and villainy can be mercilessly thin.

That leaves us with the final category: entertainers. In the 1980s and 90s, local celebrities were big both at home and abroad. While some of our stars can still pack a concert hall today, they can't escape the tsunami that has swept across the entertainment industry. Record sales and box office revenues have plummeted because of piracy and illegal downloads. Globalization and the Internet also allow consumers to seek more sophisticated choices from America, Korea and Japan at the click of a mouse. Unwilling to take financial risks, local record labels and movie studios stick to their tired formulas and churn out more of the same. The Age of the Superstar is over. What we now have is a lineup of C-list celebrities who, when stacked up against Teresa Teng and Anita Mui, seem like such wannabes.

A notable exception to our languishing entertainment industry is Andy Lau, one of the most enduring entertainers of our generation. Lau's dedication to his craft and commitment to be the best in whatever he sets his mind to do have made him the symbol of the so-called "Hong Kong spirit." His career has leapfrogged stardom into spiritual leadership. Despite persistent rumors about his personal life and occasional criticism of his acting and singing skills, the showbiz veteran keeps his head down and presses on, and in the process, has become a national hero of sorts.

The charismatic Andy Lau

I suppose if Andy Lau were to die in a plane crash tomorrow, citizens would come out in droves to pay their final respects. Nevertheless, I have my doubts that the passing of any public figure, even one like Lau, would touch us in this day and age. We think of a hero as someone who inspires us with their audacity and gives us courage to go where no one has gone before. For most of us in Hong Kong, however, our paths have been mapped out for us since the day we are born. We spend the first 30 years of our lives getting good grades and steady jobs, and the next 30 years raising our children and paying off our mortgage. The play-it-safe roadmap has filled the city with insurance agents and real estate brokers instead of writers and artists. To put it plainly, we are not in the market for inspiration. What's more, our bitterness toward the super rich, the growing distrust of our policymakers, and the general pessimism that the heyday of the Booming 80s are forever gone have spoiled our appetite for idolatry. I'm beginning to think that Alex was right: we do live in a heroless city.

Spare the Rod

Pediatricians set certain developmental milestones for children. Babies, for instance, are expected to take their first steps between nine and 12 months. Toddlers should be potty trained by age three. If a child has trouble feeding himself or tying his shoelaces by the time he reaches kindergarten, it raises a red flag for the parents. Professional help is sought and remedial steps are taken. But when an entire generation of children in Hong Kong is unable to perform the simplest of daily tasks and lacks the most basic of social skills, we shrug it off as "boys will be boys." We call them *gonghai* (港孩) in Cantonese – millennials who have been spoiled rotten by their middle class parents and are completely helpless without them. We tell ourselves that it is no big deal, that it is just a generational thing. Is it?

Children are a precious commodity in Hong Kong. According to a recent study by the World Bank, there are only 1.1 births for every woman in Hong Kong, the second lowest rate among 200 countries surveyed. The top reason cited by local parents for their reluctance to procreate is money. One economist puts the cost of raising a child at HK$4 million (US$500,000). That just about covers the cost of food, supplies, tuition from preschool to university and sundry extra-curricular activities along the way. Considering that the city's median household income is around HK$20,000 (US$2,500) a month, it is little wonder that local parents think thrice before having children, and that few dare have more than one. While we scoff at China's one child policy, the economic reality is that Hong Kong parents are in the same boat as their mainland counterparts. Deng Xiaoping, the father of population control, must be gloating in his grave.

Being a *gonghai* has its perks. He (or she) wallows in middle class abundance: toys, books and state of the art electronics. As part of the "Trophy Generation," he grows up having his shoulder patted and his ego fed. Efforts are mistaken for skills and medals are given out just for showing up. However, it is the access to cheap domestic help that has turned these princelings into pint-sized tyrants. The little emperor barks orders at his caretaker whenever his finger nails need a trim or his fish requires deboning. He is Veruca Salt after she finds out she hasn't won the golden ticket to the chocolate factory. For who would bother with "please" and "thank you" when he can get away with "I want it NOW"?

The combination of doting parents and domestic helpers have made our children, who are otherwise mentally sound, incapable of looking after themselves. We have coined the phrase "high marks, low smarts" to describe a local child who gets straight 'A's in school but can't brush his own teeth at home. *Gonghai* stories are popular on social media because they make good party jokes. One urban legend involves a child who doodled on $100 bills thinking that it was scrap paper. Another one tells the tale of a young cook who forgot to take the noodles out of the plastic wrapping before dropping the whole thing into a pot of boiling water. Sadly, his parents probably found it incredibly cute and proceeded to post the video on YouTube.

It takes two to feed a six-year-old

The sheltered environment at home, and the sense of entitlement it instills, are setting our children up to fail in the real world. In the not-so-distant future, the trophy kid will discover to his absolute horror that the daily grind of a desk job bears little resemblance to the bubble in which he grew up. But he is not panicking just yet, because he knows the parents will always be there to catch his fall. There will be a hot meal and a warm bed waiting for him at home. Things will get dicey, however, when Peter Pan finally decides to cut the umbilical cord. He will get married and move into his own place (down payment courtesy of mom and dad), only to find out that his spouse is an exact mirror image of himself. Putting two *gonghai* under the same roof is to have the blind leading the blind. Who does laundry and how much water does a cup of rice need? How can any argument be resolved if neither person listens and both think they are always right?

It was only a generation ago that the city was a very different place. People born in the 1960s and 70s – like my siblings and I – were raised in a sink or swim environment. Hong Kong was still an emerging market and most families muddled through with what little they had. Left to our own devices, Gen X children grew up doing everything themselves: cooking meals, making their own beds and fixing the toilet flush. Domestic help was reserved for the upper class – there were always a handful of privileged kids in every school who got dropped off and picked up by their maids. Back then families were much larger, which provided both companionship and competition. We wore hand-me-downs and played with the same toys until they broke. The home doubled as a classroom where social skills were honed and life lessons learned. We turned out all right.

It is therefore all the more surprising that when it is our turn to have a family, we throw away everything we learned from our childhood. We suddenly morph into "helicopter parents," so called because they hover over their kids and intervene at the first sign of trouble. In Cantonese, we borrow the Japanese term "monster parents" to refer to those who threaten teachers who give their children bad grades and – this is a real story – demand the government to send a chartered plane to pick up their kids from London after a snowstorm has led to the cancellation of their flights. It makes you wonder: how did the same people who reminisce about their old-fashioned upbringing become such over-protective parents?

I can think of two explanations. The first is that we can't bear to see our kids go through the hardship we ourselves went through. We live by the motto: "We work hard so they don't have to."

Time has changed and we don't need them doing chores like Cinderella any more. We pile on the extracurricular activities to help them reach their full potential and get into better schools. Our intentions are noble.

Or so they seem until we scratch beneath the surface to reveal the second, and less honorable, explanation. Deep down inside, some of us are still fighting our childhood demons – wounds from decades ago that have yet to heal. Somewhere in those halcyon days of youth, when we were doing dishes in the kitchen or saving up lunch money for a pair of sneakers, we knew we could do better for ourselves. We wanted to learn a musical instrument and take our sports seriously, as did the privileged kids we knew, but the opportunities escaped us. By the time we could afford all those things, the train had already left the station. We are too old to be good at anything other than making money.

While it is too late for us, it is not too late for our children. So we pack their timetable with violin practices and tennis classes. We speak English to them in public and even make them learn some French. They will succeed where we have failed. Our children, the reincarnation of our idealized selves, will be our ultimate redemption.

In the end it is not *them*, it is *us*. The spoiled brats are merely victims of our own inadequacy. We shield them from the hardship of life not because they can't handle it, but because we think they are too good for it. We let them behave badly not because they should, but because they can. The *gonghai* phenomenon lays bare the misguided notion that incompetence and character flaws are a luxury that only the upper class is afforded and that our children have finally joined the ranks of the privileged. It's time we got over ourselves so our children can live their own lives.

The King and I

I always find business trips a great way to catch up on the movies I have missed. On my way to a meeting in Jakarta a few weeks ago, I was thrilled to find on the in-flight entertainment menu *The King's Speech*, the low budget British history drama that came out of nowhere but went on to clinch four top awards at the Oscars. The film tells the story of King George VI, a lifelong stutterer who struggled to overcome his crippling speech impediment with the help of an unorthodox Australian speech therapist. David Seidler, who wrote the screenplay for the film, was himself a stutterer as a child and used to listen to George VI's wartime speeches on the radio as a source of inspiration. With the help of seasoned actors Colin Firth and Geoffrey Rush, Seidler turned an otherwise little known king into a courageous hero who was able to galvanize his nation in turbulent times and, in doing so, gave eloquent voice to the stuttering community around the world.

* * *

When I was a child I hated meeting new people. The first thing I had to say to a stranger was my name. And I hated saying my name, for the "j" sound was the most difficult of them all. No matter how many times I rehearsed it in my head, I always ended up sounding like a sputtering engine. Simple day to day tasks like answering the phone would cause me great anxiety and humiliation. When my uncle named me at birth, he had no idea that the innocent name he picked would create such trouble for his baby nephew.

Over the years, I learned to choose the path of least resistance by paraphrasing, modifying and self-editing. I would avoid words and phrases that were hard to say and substitute them with easier ones. I spent my spare time making up new, inventive ways to get my words out. For instance, stomping my feet or swinging my body sometimes helped. Like other stutterers, I learned to adapt, for adaptation is the only way to survive in an impatient world.

At home my brothers and sisters, even my parents, would make fun of my stutter. I used to tell myself that it was the Chinese way of saying "It's no big deal. We love you the way you are." It probably was. Steeped in Chinese folklore, my mom would tell me that people with thin lips, like my brother Dan, were blessed with eloquence and would make great orators and politicians. I, on the other hand, had fat lips and when I grew up I should stick to professions that required more thinking than talking. An engineer or an accountant perhaps. I took my mother's career advice to heart and mentally crossed out lawyer and teacher from the list. Like other stutterers, I learned to accept, for acceptance is the only way to survive in an unfair world.

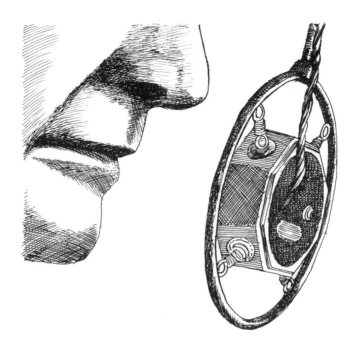

*What comes naturally to most people
can be the scariest thing for some*

Stuttering is a behavioral disorder defined by the World Health Organization as "a recurrent speech impediment characterized by frequent repetition or prolongation of sounds." There are reportedly 68 million stutterers in the world, around 1% of the general population. They live under constant stress, caused by even the simplest of social interactions where shame is the knife and the scars run deep. The disfluent man is destined to lead a life of missed opportunities and unrequited attention.

Like people afflicted with other physical disabilities, stutterers often struggle with their handicap on their own. Encouragement from parents and peers often makes the speaker feel even more self-conscious. Studies show that roughly 75% of stuttering children recover by their early teens. The remaining 25%, however, carry their speech impediment to adulthood and show little improvement despite therapy and medication. Nevertheless, there appears to be no shortage of famous and successful stuttering adults past and present, from Isaac Newton and Winston Churchill to Marilyn Monroe and James Earl Jones. Stutterers' organizations and support groups hold up their pictures as evidence that even disfluent people can lead happy, fulfilled lives.

Thankfully I am among the 75% of the stuttering population who recover from their childhood stammer. My disfluency began to fall away during university and, by the time I was in law school, I had all but conquered my fear of speaking in public. Being among outspoken law students every day for three years enabled me to pretend I was one of them, while I secretly observed the way they talked and learned by osmosis. Just like that, the biggest source of embarrassment throughout my adolescence became a thing of the past. Still, even today, my stutter creeps back every once in a while. I find myself lapsing into my old stammer when my confidence is most shaken, such as when telling an unconvincing lie or speaking French or Mandarin.

Many years have gone by since my stuttering days. I now practice law full time and teach English on weekends, the two very things that I had crossed off from my list – things that I had once considered off limits for a person with my limitations. I decided to go to law school despite, and because of, my limitations, not so much as an act of defiance to prove my mom wrong as a flash of boyish chivalry to prove myself right. I came to realize that there was a bigger lesson hidden somewhere in the story: how often do we build walls around ourselves by crossing things off our lists and accepting limitations that either can be overcome or never existed in the first place?

*   *   *

I arrived at my meeting in Jakarta, in a room full of strangers. Those same serious faces and business suits. I introduced myself and my team and proceeded to chair the all-day meeting with equal parts ease and confidence. Public speaking – the most dreaded of all human experiences to many people – no longer intimidates me. It empowers me and reminds me how far I have come to get to where I am. "You have such perseverance, Bertie, you are the bravest man I know," Lionel Logue, the Australian speech therapist, tells King George VI in one of the most moving dialogues in *The King's Speech*. Even though achieving normal fluency is nothing that the general population would brag about, I have always considered it one of my proudest achievements.

我的藝術家爸爸

My Father the Artist

When I was little, what my father did for a living was a mystery to my friends. Whenever I had to fill out a personal data form in school, I would put down "artist" under "Father's occupation." In the minds of my teachers and classmates, my dad could have been an oil painter, a Canto pop idol or someone who worked at a tattoo parlor. He was of course none of those things.

It wasn't until I was older that I learned the word "illustrator" and was able to properly explain what my father did: he drew pictures for martial arts and romance serials that appeared in daily newspapers. But clarity comes with its problems. My friends would ask me to show them my dad's work, which was all well and good except that many of the stories he illustrated were erotic, and some were altogether pornographic. So I went back to calling my father an artist. If some of my friends mistook him for a singer or tattooist, then so be it.

Self-portrait, drawn in 2013

My father worked at home. For as long as I could remember, he was always slouching over his desk and working his paint brushes under an incandescent light bulb like a concert pianist in the spotlight. My parents' bedroom doubled as his studio – the earliest version of a home office. To expand his work surface, he lay on top of his small desk a piece of plywood, which was held down by ink bottles and sundry notebooks. We knew better than to rest our elbows on the board or else everything would topple over. His desk was as messy as a wet market. There were brushes and pencils and rulers and French curves. Old newspaper clippings interlaced with non-winning lottery tickets. Somehow he knew exactly where things were. There was order in his ink-stained chaos.

Every night, serial writers would telephone my father to tell him what to draw for their next installments. Mysterious voices would leak from the telephone handset, spilling chains of cryptic words:

"Iron Crane crosses swords with the traitor who murdered his master, only to find himself out-skilled."

"The star-crossed lovers discover their true identity as siblings and decide to swallow poison."

"Bao Yu slowly undoes the young maiden's blouse and begins running his fingers..."

My father would write down these verbal cues at an astounding speed. He used a type of shorthand that only he could understand. The writers never had to explain the same thing twice and he never had to call them back.

Once, my dad was in the bathroom when one of the writers called. My sister Ada, who is only a few years older than me, answered the phone and started scribbling on dad's notebook, unfazed by the tremendous responsibility. After she hung up, I walked over to the desk to see what she had written. The first sentence read:

YY 闖入少林寺

It meant YY stormed into a Shaolin Temple. YY is the famous Japanese sports brand Yonex that makes badminton rackets. After my father returned to his desk, I asked him how he planned to draw a racket flying into a monastery. He had a chuckle and explained that "YY" was just my sister's shorthand for Yeung Ying, the name of a famous kung fu character. I was impressed not only by Ada's quick wit, but also by how ready she was to step into my father's place. Perhaps one day I could too.

Based on the cues in his notebook, my dad would begin his composition. He would outline the scene using a light blue pencil so that the sketch wouldn't show up on the drawings when they went to print. Back then, all the newspapers were in black and white and so all he would need was a jar of black ink, a few paint brushes and a set of steel-tipped pens for finer details. There was always a small jar of white ink within reach in case he needed to correct an error. I always thought that he should have patented the idea before BIC stole it and started selling White Out fluids.

Once the drawings were done, someone needed to deliver them to the newspapers. My father drew for about a dozen daily papers, but only one of them had hired a messenger to pick up the drawings from our home. Each night, a leather clad man would ring our door bell at around ten o'clock when all the good kids were already in bed. The messenger traveled by motorcycle – at least that's what we guessed based on the watermelon-sized helmet tucked under his arm. If his helmet was wet, we knew it had been raining outside. If the helmet smelled like burned grass, we knew he had had a cigarette before coming up. In front of the messenger, we would always address him with the honorific "Uncle." Behind his back, we just called him "Pickup Dude."

Pickup Dude was much more than a messenger, he was an alarm clock. Procrastination is a trait that runs in the family, and my father always left things to the last minute. He would spend all night playing with his Casio game calculator until the ominous doorbell would ring and the whole family would scream in unison, "Pickup Dude is here!!" That was my dad's cue to put down his game and finish his drawings. The rest of us would take turns keeping the messenger busy as a way to divert his attention. We would turn on the television, offer him cold drinks and make him play computer games.

So every night we entertained Pickup Dude like a VIP, all to buy my father some time. My younger brother Dan would say, "Uncle, please take a seat" while I offered, "Which game would you like to play tonight, Uncle?" One night, however, Dan forgot his manners and kept hogging the computer. That's when I blurted out: "Don't be rude and let Pickup Dude play!" Everyone froze in horror as the guest discovered his unflattering alias. When a different messenger showed up a few weeks after the incident, I wondered if Pickup Dude had asked for a reassignment because of my slip-up.

For the rest of the newspapers, we had to do the leg work ourselves. When all of us were still small, my mother would make the deliveries. Her newspaper route covered all of Hong Kong Island, from the *Ming Pao Daily* in Quarry Bay to *Ta Kung Pao* in Wanchai and *Sing Tao* in Central. As the children came of age, my mom passed the baton to my older brother and sisters. And when they became too busy with public exams, the responsibility fell on Dan and me. It was a relay race that spanned two generations.

Being an errand boy was exciting at the beginning, because not many 10-year-olds get to go out at night and explore the city unaccompanied. I would visit the record store in Wanchai, hang out at the bookshop in Causeway Bay and peek into the scary funeral home in North Point. I would memorize street names and observe strangers on the streets. There was the old lady who talked to herself while picking through the trash, the storekeeper's daughter who acted out scenes from unknown plays, and teenagers who walked up and down the block because they didn't want to go home. Sometimes I wondered what they thought of me when they saw a skinny boy with a bowl haircut loitering with an envelope in his hand.

For some reason, my dad always left the *Chiu Yin Daily* drawing till the end of the day. The newspaper's office was in Causeway Bay and he would give us HK$5 (US$0.65) to take the taxi because it was late at night. He taught us how to instruct the cab driver: "Just tell the taxi uncle to take the expressway to Causeway Bay and make a left on Percival Street." Easy peasy. I was doing all right until one time when my limited conversational skills caught up with me.

"Where to, kid?"

"Take the expressway to Causeway Bay and make a left on Percival Street."

"You didn't shut the door completely, kid."

"Take the expressway to Causeway Bay and make a left on Percival Street."

The good thing about taking the taxi was that I didn't have to actually take the taxi. If the bus arrived before a cab did, I would hop onto the double decker (which cost HK$1.20) and keep the taxi fare. It made the most sense during rainy nights when all the taxis would suddenly disappear. Back then HK$5 stretched far — it felt like HK$500 today. The savings would all go to the Jason Ng Sneaker Fund.

The novelty of running night errands wore off after a few months. There were deliveries to be made every single evening, whether it was a school night, a public holiday or the day before a final exam. Dan and I alternated but sometimes *both* of us were too busy to go. That inevitably led to arguments over who had more school work, whose grades were more at stake and whose future took priority. My father would sit quietly by and watch the two of us go at each other. Then suddenly, he would leap out of his chair and start changing out of his pajamas. He would put on his watch, tuck the drawings inside his jacket and walk out of the house without a word. Dan and I called it his "trump card," a dramatic move designed to make us feel guilty about shirking our filial duty. When he returned a couple of hours later, he wouldn't talk to either of us for the rest of the night. My brother and I would feel bad, although in truth we were relieved that we had escaped the chore. Over time we got used to his theatrics and just let it happen. On average, he would use the trump card two, three times a month.

There were a lot of things I didn't understand as a child. What my father did for a living and, more importantly, why. I wished he were an accountant, a teacher or anyone with a more normal occupation. I wished he hadn't chosen a job that kept him at home all day like a prisoner, or turned us into child laborers when all the other kids were home studying. Somewhere in my childhood, when I was most resentful, I vowed never to do what my father did.

Decades flew by in the blink of an eye. My father is long retired and now lives in Toronto with my mom. We often speak of the old days in Hong Kong and how he had raised five children on a freelance job and hadn't taken a vacation in decades. I tell him that Dan and I used to conspire to make him use his trump card so we could get out of the chore. We can all laugh about it now.

As for me, I now moonlight as a freelance writer. Each time I find myself writing into the small hours of the night, I will smile to myself at the irony of it all. I procrastinate like my father and struggle to meet deadlines like him. I spend all my free time slouching over my messy desk at home the same way he did for 35 years. The more I didn't want his life, it seems, the more I ended up living it. It makes me wonder if I am destined to do what I do. Perhaps spending all those evenings on the streets as a delivery boy had opened my eyes to the iridescent city I now write about. I may not have had the childhood every kid wants, but I wouldn't trade it for the world.

Adapted from the essay Delivering Drawings *(《交稿》) by Daniel Y. Ng.*

長
憂
九
十
九

Ninety-nine Years of Worry

This November my parents will celebrate their 25th year in Canada. For two and a half decades, they have lived out their retirement dream in a quiet Toronto suburb, a world away from the humdrum city life they left behind in Hong Kong. Scattered around the world, their five children and half-dozen grandchildren take turns visiting them. I, for instance, take the 16-hour trans-Pacific flight from Hong Kong to spend a week with them every winter. In their house, they have kept my room the way I left it 15 years ago. When I go to the kitchen, I will see my name written on the wall calendar in bright red ink, with a squiggly line that runs across the days of my visit.

When I am in Hong Kong, I am supposed to call my parents twice a month. There is always an excuse not to: the twelve-hour time difference (or is it thirteen?), my travel schedule, a writing streak that cannot be interrupted. It doesn't bother my dad nearly as much as it does my mom. Indeed, every phone call she picks up begins with the same question: "Why do you never call?" To make up for it, I try to buy her something nice each time I see her. Two years ago I got her a handbag she only uses twice a year; last Christmas it was a bracelet that ended up in the safety deposit box. Between my siblings and me, we have managed to stuff her closet with gifts, some of them have never been used and are still in their original shopping bags.

Although my mom has everything she needs and wants very little else, she is constantly worried. She isn't worried about money. "I have lots saved up," she keeps telling us. And she isn't worried about her health. "I am built like a horse," she will joke. Instead, she worries about her five very grown up children, the oldest of whom turned 50 last year. Take me for example. She worries that I work too much, spend too much and eat out too much. I don't sleep enough, save enough or call her enough. It is as though from the first breath I took until the last one she draws, she is committed to being the Worrier-in-Chief, whose battle cry goes something like: Don't slouch and eat your vegetables!

For a long time I knew very little about my mother's past and what she was like before she became, well, Mom. I decided to remedy that during my last visit to Toronto and sat down with her for an interview. I picked an afternoon when my dad was out with his friends so she would feel less inhibited. I told her half-jokingly that someday I might write a story about her. To my surprise, she agreed, as if she had been waiting for the invitation for years. Like the old lady in *Titanic*, she began to recount her storied past.

"I am the oldest daughter of my father's second wife," she opened. It could have been the first line of a Russian novel.

My mom and her two oldest children, taken in 1965

My mom was born into a wealthy landowner's family in Toishan (台山), a town near Guangzhou. Before the Communists "liberated" China in 1949, she was a spoiled brat with young maids at her beck and call. "I would pinch them whenever they disobeyed me," she recalled, while checking her unmanicured nails despite herself. Her father's untimely death, followed by sweeping land reforms in the 1950s, took everything away. Overnight the spoiled brat became a hardened teenager who had to grow up fast. She survived by selling what was left at home: vases, furniture and anything else of any value. At age 21, she made the most daring decision of her life: she dropped out of teachers' college and fled to Hong Kong. She found part time work as a proofreader at a local newspaper, where she would meet her future husband.

"You look pretty," I said to my mom while we flipped through her old pictures in the bedroom. "Gosh no, not at all," she denied. It wasn't modesty as much as pride. "I was plain compared to your dad. He was a real knockout." Good-looking as he was, my father has always had a bad limp because of a childhood polio affliction. Relatives repeatedly told my mom not to fall for the "cripple." She didn't listen and went on to marry him a few years later. "Everyone told me I was making a big mistake," she smirked, "but love is blind." That was the first time I heard my mom speak so candidly about love. It was also the first time I realized that it was her act of defiance that brought me into this world.

That afternoon my mom and I talked for hours, the longest we had spoken in years. Her spirited narrative, interrupted by an occasional girly giggle, breathed life into the still photographs taken in a different time and a different world. Who would have guessed that this porcelain doll face in black and white, a hopeless romantic who married for love instead of money, would be the same worrywart who tells me to go to bed at eleven and asks if I have my passport before I head to the airport?

During the 1960s and 70s, most families in Hong Kong made do with very little. People made their own clothes, eating out was rare and the "middle class" was a foreign concept. My parents had to run a tight ship to raise five children. "My friends were amazed at how I managed with the little money your father gave me every month," my mom said. One of them helped her purchase a sewing machine on installment so she could make a few extra bucks on the side. That explains all those tiny Barbie doll dresses stacked neatly in the middle of the living room when I was little. "They pay for your schoolbooks," she would tell us so that we wouldn't mess them up. I still remember the sound of the cast iron wheel spinning to the rhythm of her foot pedal.

Though my mom barely scraped by, what little she had left she used to help out her relatives in Toishan. During the Cultural Revolution, there were widespread food shortages in China. Carbohydrates and fat were badly needed to fight malnutrition, jaundice and other diseases. Twice a month she visited the neighborhood pharmacy that offered courier services to China. Post offices on the mainland were known to open packages from Hong Kong on the pretext of counter-subversion, but really just to make off with what was inside. That's why my mom never sent any money – it would just get "lost." She didn't send rice or flour either because they were too heavy and not nutritious enough. Instead, she would buy a half-dozen loaves of bread, soak them in syrup or oil, and dry them in the sun so that they became much lighter and could be stored for weeks. I asked who taught her to do a thing like that. "That's what everyone else did. You just knew," she replied.

In the 1980s after the Shenzhen border opened up, she continued to send clothes, shoes and other household supplies to her relatives back home. In their eyes my mom was the rich aunt in Hong Kong who put five children through college and still had money to spare. Wealth and sustenance, she had learned, were such relative terms.

Going against the grain of society, my mom never bothered to take her husband's last name. She kept her maiden name Louie (雷), which literally means "thunder" in Chinese. As a kid I was convinced that her forbidding name was the reason for her short temper. While other mothers nagged, mine liked to scream. If one of us overslept by a few minutes on a school day or ate a candy bar before dinner, she would come down on the miscreant with a scolding that would make Amy Chua's tiger mom look like a pussy cat. Cross her on a steamy summer day and we were guaranteed a good spanking. Her weapon of choice was any household object with a hard edge. We all learned at a young age to do exactly as she said and stay out of her way. Tantrums never worked and always backfired, for in the House of Thunder the squeaky wheel got not the oil but flog marks on the thigh.

My mom's tough love was matched by her nerves of steel. Things that instill universal fear among mortals, such as household pests, did not stand a chance against her. She was known to pick up a spider with her bare toes and drop it into the toilet. Geckos that send chills down everyone's spine are "our friends" and she would shoo them away like they were pets. "You should see those giant blood sucking leeches back in Toishan," she would tell us while we squirmed in the corner.

Once, we found out to our absolute horror that there was a beehive inside the bedroom air-conditioner. Instead of calling an exterminator (which to her would have been both a waste of money and a cop out), she suited herself up in plastic bags and duct tape, and entered the bedroom for a bare knuckle fight with an enemy that outnumbered her 200 to one. She smashed the hive with a broomstick and pushed back the charging army of angry bees with a canister of bug spray. When Suzanne Collins crafted her heroine in *The Hunger Games*, she might have had this Toishanese woman in mind.

I was a handful as a child. I was prone to all sorts of illnesses and diseases, from measles and chicken pox to asthma and an obligatory case of flu whenever the temperature dipped below a certain point. The flu would then turn into a cough and the cough into more asthma attacks. It was an endless cycle of sickness and convalescence, all at my mom's expense. To make things harder still, I was a pathologically picky eater who greeted every meal with a long face and sealed lips. My mom used to complain that I was more work than the other four children combined.

If there was a silver lining to my sickly childhood, it was that my poor health brought the two of us closer. Between all the doctor's visits, the x-rays and the blood tests, we wound up spending a good deal of time together. Whether it was to kill time or to distract me from the pain I was in, she never missed a chance to dispense a dose of motherly advice on life. She would tell me that, considering all the close calls I had with my health, I owed a big debt to the gods to which she prayed. I should therefore always give generously to those in need. At the time it sounded like the kind of thing any mother would say to her children. Though with everything I now know about her past, those words have taken on new meaning. I suspect she went to such great lengths to help her relatives in Toishan because she too had a big debt to repay – the fact that she fled China just in time and beat the odds to marry the love of her life. Above all, she has five children who love her and hang on her every word, even though they don't always like to admit it.

There is a Chinese saying: A person who lives to 100 keeps his parents worried for 99 years. It is true, mothers never stop worrying. It is their job. But it is also the son's job to tell his mother that everything is all right. All the presents I have given my mom, things that she doesn't need, have nothing to do with my guilt for not calling her enough. Instead, they are displays of largesse and generosity – a declaration that "See, mom, I'm doing fine. So please stop worrying about me." Likewise, it is possible that her constant worrying is her roundabout way of telling me that she, too, is doing fine. For how else would she have the time and energy to fuss over every minute detail of her children's lives? All these years mother and son have been swept up in a complicated dance of love and reticence, each aching to reassure the other of their happy existence. Despite the different worlds we live in, the two of us share a common belief that there is no greater gift in this world than the knowledge that someone you care about is living well. Everything else, like handbags and bracelets, is a poor substitute.

By the same author:

HONG KONG State of Mind
ISBN 978-988-19003-1-9

Hong Kong is a mixed bag of a city. It is where Mercedes outnumber taxi cabs, partygoers count down to Christmas every December 24, and larger-than-life billboards of fortune tellers and cram school tutors compete with breathtaking skylines.

HONG KONG State of Mind is a collection of essays by a popular blogger who zeroes in on the city's idiosyncrasies with deadpan precision. At once an outsider looking in and an insider looking out, Jason Y. Ng has created something for everyone: a travel journal for the passing visitor, a user's manual for the wide-eyed expat, and an open diary for the native Hong Konger looking for moments of reflection.

Umbrellas in Bloom

ISBN 978-988-13765-3-4

The Umbrella Movement put Hong Kong on the world map and elevated a docile, money-minded Asian island to a model for pro-democracy campaigns across the globe. *Umbrellas in Bloom* is the first book available in English to chronicle this history-making event, written by a bestselling author and columnist based on his firsthand account at the main protest sites.

Ng takes a no-holds-barred, fly-on-the-wall approach to covering politics. *Umbrellas in Bloom* steps through the 79-day struggle, from the firing of the first shot of tear gas by riot police to the evacuation of the last protester from the downtown encampments. It is all you need to know about the occupy movement: who took part in it, why it happened, how it transpired, and what it did and did not achieve.

With forewords by Joshua Wong and Chip Tsao.

JOIN JASON Y. NG AND OTHER SHARK SAVERS
who are FINished with FINs.
Take the pledge at *www.FinishedWithFins.org*.

I'm FINished
WITH FINS
一翅都唔食

Markus Shaw
邵在德
Shaw Group
邵氏集團

Jennifer Tse
謝婷婷
Actress
藝人

Real Ting
丁子高
PR
資深公關

Tanya Chan
陳淑莊
Vice Chairman (External Affair)
Of Civic Party
公民黨外務副主席

Jason Y. Ng
Author/Columnist
作者/專欄作家

Sharon Kwok
郭秀雲
Founder, AquaMeridian
Conservation &
Education Foundation
海峰環保教育基金創辦人

Alex Fong
方力申
Singer/Actor
歌手/藝人

G.E.M.
鄧紫棋
Singer
歌手

Anthony Wong
黃耀明
Singer
歌手

Official Campaign Partners:

SHARK SAVERS 護鯊行動 HONG KONG | WWF | 60+ | WILDAID 野生救援 | NATIONAL GEOGRAPHIC CHANNEL | NAT GEO WILD

加入我們，立即承諾
Join us, take your
pledge online:
www.FinishedWithFins.org